PHP Security and Session Management

*Managing Sessions and Ensuring PHP Security
(2022 Guide for Beginners)*

Ray Dinwiddie

Table of Contents

Overview of PHP Security

The internet is a major component of the modern world, and all the information about multinational corporations' products can be found online.

In this book, we'll talk about how our data is insecure and how vulnerable sensitive data on the internet is. Who are the attackers, and how do they intend to get our private information?

Several security breaches will be exposed throughout the book, along with the efforts that have been done and those that still need to be taken to protect our data.

The main focus of the book is on discussing numerous risks to data acquisition, PHP security's role in this area and the crucial steps PHP security has taken to address these problems. The most typical dangers to data security will be covered in the first chapter, along with the most fundamental methods for defending against them. Are they secure? is the fundamental query here. What particular security-related steps have been taken?

The possibility of attacks on websites and email accounts is growing.

the increase in phishing, a scam where web users are misled into providing criminals with their personal information. This is accomplished by creating phony documents, like bank or credit card statements, that seem to have come from reliable sources. They are sent through emails that attempt to look like they are coming from the real sender.

Links from governmental organizations and spam/junk mail from other people's spam lists are examples of these. When you receive an email or text message from one of these people, it's not that person sending you the message; rather, it's that computer virus file that has uploaded all of these messages to the network after these hackers hacked into your system and obtained sensitive information or files you weren't even aware were even there. These facts demonstrate the lack of security in our large data and, more crucially, our professional data. However, let's examine the security of the data that we publish on social media. This is a genuinely perplexing question.

Because the information we share is frequently accessible to third parties, who may even alter it, This gives you the sense that your website page is hiding something unsavory or harmful. You are exposed to anyone with unrestricted access to your private information, regardless of how much that person wants to utilize those files for any purpose because your email address and all associated information are saved in those same files. We shall see here the major sort of attacker that attacks our data. Our entire internet infrastructure is insecure, and did we ever notice who was stealing our sensitive data?

Numerous persons working on various layers can access our data. A "malicious URL" attack is the most common kind of attacker. It indicates that the target has reached a malicious website after clicking on an unwelcome link. Therefore, if a hacker sends you an email asking you to click on a link, he intends to steal your login information, provide you with a weak password, and send your information to his computer and password recovery software.

Following that, he will change your passwords and send you another email advising you to visit the website where he took everything. How they obtain our info is the next thought that comes to mind.

The use of social engineering is a frequent method of stealing data and your identity. A good illustration is asking someone you've met online or who is familiar with you for money. When you opt to get a subscription to your preferred sports team, it is frequently the simplest approach to obtain your social security number or whatever else you are willing to put on the line.

Because most potential victims have little to no computer skills, social engineering is effective. The majority of folks who lack fundamental computer literacy aren't very concerned about being duped into clicking on a phishing link. Since of this, it is challenging for attackers to win over a large number of targets because they must make victims feel uneasy enough to prevent them from losing faith in other people.

If you are more tech-savvy or have a lot of useful information on your profile that would be simple to steal, or if you are someone with loads of important information, phishing is frequently the most successful way to get access to an account over a network.

It can happen occasionally when a victim isn't necessarily aware that something illegal is going on online (although these threats typically disappear without being noticed). Even if you notice questionable activity, you might not even be aware of it. These kinds of weaknesses are simpler for thieves to take advantage of than new strategies for deceiving you.

One of the first things the FBI does after receiving a notification is to begin an investigation. In other words, Verizon Wireless will look into and treat seriously any email that purports to be from that company that is sent to you. Let's say Verizon Wireless doesn't consider it important. In that situation, that's where things start to get serious because Verizon is now focusing on something that it shouldn't be doing and may potentially be acting improperly. Every day, there are millions of these scams out there, and it's not simply a problem for companies. Likewise, people are falling for them.

An imposter can contact you if someone complains that they are getting demands for cash or things. The customer calls the store management to inform them that he wants 10 pounds of beefsteak chicken for supper because you think, "maybe I should make a sale here." Or he'll give them a call a few days before Thanksgiving and offer, "Hey, how about buying two big bottles of wine?" You'll see him pick up several boxes and sell them right away if that's the case.

Most likely, the person you're meeting on a dating site isn't to blame if your life has been stolen. The only reason someone is on your website is so you can place an advertisement and let them know they are interested in everything and everything that comes into your inbox.

Let's now examine the required steps that can be made to resolve these funny problems.

Avoid opening any attached files unless you are certain that the links you are viewing are trustworthy if you want to stop these impostors from taking advantage of you. You should never open attachments while accessing any other files because this usually only relates to phishing links. Never click on any links unless you are certain that they are trustworthy, such as those coming from a reputable source like your bank account. It's not a good idea to allow yourself to be taken advantage of unless you have adequate security measures in place, such as a bank account.

The biggest and most used programming language for cloud applications is PHP. W3Techs analysis from April 2019 shows that 79 percent of websites use PHP. These websites include, among others, Encyclopedia, Google, and LinkedIn. PHP security is essential because PHP is used so widely and so many PHP apps are weak. PHP is an effective tool for handling these situations. Let's look at some other possibilities and how they might give the attacker access to our data.

require File.expand_path("../
abort("The Rails environment
require 'spec_helper'
require 'rspec/rails'
require 'capybara/rspec'
require 'capybara/rails'
Capybara.javascript_driver =
Category.delete_all; Category
Shoulda::Matchers.configure
config.integrate
with.test_framework :rspec
with.library :rails
end
end
Add additional

Chapter 1

XSS ATTEMPTED

A type of attack known as XSS is caused by a remote location application that is only present on the client side. Destructive JavaScript is being attempted to be activated in a web page application. A computer virus that was introduced by the program or online application strikes the original webpage.

The user visits a website or a surface program with a virus embedded in it, and it eventually hunts the user's data. That could be transmitted to the computer and lead to significant issues. A website or online application can install malicious software on a user's computer. Attacks using pass scripts are frequently used against websites and delivered messages that share a common context.

If a new website or web app generates content that uses sanitized input validation, it may be vulnerable to cross-site scripting. This dynamic material must then be parsed by the server. As an illustration, XSS flaws can be found in Visual Studio code, Ajax, Swf, and even Xhtml. Given that JavaScript is necessary for the majority of web interactions, it might be argued that they are most prevalent in JavaScript. Should cross-site scripting occur, and who is to blame if not the user?

Therefore, even if an aggressor were to use an insecure web server or a website with weak security, its users would still be at risk. An attacker might use this flaw on a website to run PHP on a web device. Cross-site scripting and other security threats are not the user's fault. If it affects your users, it also affects you. Instead of serving the needs of the customer, inter programming can be used to vandalize a website.

Hackers can employ infected scripts to alter the web's structure or even redirect users to risky websites that are tainted with malware. The backend procedural code that follows can be used to show the majority of preceding statements on a web page.

```
print  "<html>" print  "<h1>Most  recent  comment</h1>"
print
database. latest Comment print "</html>"
<html>         <h1>Most         recent         comment</h1>
<script>doSomethingEvil();
</script> </html>
```

The application mentioned above just displays the most recent post from a dataset on an HTML document. There are no HTML tags or other coding in the written comment, which is thought to be text alone. Since an attacker may potentially say anything positive via a computer virus, it is indeed vulnerable to XSS. Because of its very effective invalided composites, " XSS" is challenging to circumvent.

The environment that uses user input and the programming framework has an impact on the type of XSS vulnerability and the preventative measures. However, there are a few fundamental conceptual parameters to take into account while creating a secure web application.

The remaining chapters of this book will cover XSS and all of the strategies, tactics, and crucial tasks used to address it.

HIJACKING A SESSION

The Session Hijacking attack uses the internet windows technique of management, which is frequently applied to a public key. Since HTML releases a lot of separate Port scans in return, the web service needs a way to identify every customer's connections. The Web service gives a token to a web application after a user's authentication is successful; this is the most practical approach. The URLs, web headers used as a passcode, various sections of the HTTP status header, and the web socket content are all possible locations for a session id. A buffer overflow (bridge shooting) strategy is employed to provide the identifying information whenever an intruder transmits a bogus identification to such a victim. The application uses a Way vector to automatically reveal the data contents for the current event; a custom Script could also be created using the same method and used to send the information to the attacker.

SCRIPT Warning (document. cookie)

SCRIPT

The Hijacking assault operates in this manner; we will see it thoroughly in the next chapters.

Injection

Injections are one of the most prevalent and dangerous online application hazards, leading to process failure, data loss, backup and recovery loss, and data theft. In most cases, a lack of user authentication input results in injection vulnerabilities. What can you do to reduce these attacks of hatred? It is without a doubt a premeditated strategy for handling the situation and accurately evaluating it. Avoiding SQL injection problems is easy. Alternately, programmers must either stop creating particularly problematic code or make sure that potentially dangerous SQL in user input does not affect the logic of the run search.

Popular injectable attacks include application servers, bridge programming, code injection, software Metasploit, site signature fillers, and others. Injector vulnerabilities account for a sizable portion of web app issues.

The aforementioned circumstances make it clear that we must develop defense systems to counter some of these threats.

These are your only real choices for stopping these assaults. There are two anti-injection strategies suggested by "The Open Web Application Security Project." These methods can be applied to other computer programmers in addition to SQL coding.

THE FOLLOWING PROTECTION TECHNIQUES SHOULD BE USED TO KEEP YOUR WEB SERVICES SAFE FROM INJECTION ATTACKS:

Major Challenges: Parameterized Query-Prepared Remarks

Utilization of Methods That Have Been Used Before White People's Choice List

Additional obstacles Validating Input Without Using Consumer Information

Using the White List Authentication Mechanism as an Additional Barrier, Enforcing Lowest Priority The analysis of these attacks and the security of the website can be improved with the use of additional protections like access control and data surveillance.

THE FOLLOWING SECURITY RISKS ARE XSRF AND CSRF.

A very well-known and efficient security system is XSRF or CSRF. A web app can manipulate how successfully a computer connects to a legitimate web app using a web-hosted app attack.

Various exploits are possible when web services transmit specified types of generated significance with each access to a page. That kind of hack, which makes use of the user's pre-approval connection, is also known as identity surfing or merely a one-click exploitation.

While login in to forms confirmation is necessary. The system accepts the client's identification and provides an authentication card in response. This service is weak because it uses a reliable and regularly used database to validate any query.

Visitor accesses the phony website on which fraud is taking place. WW.webhack.attacking is a malicious website.

The user has chosen to submit the option. The identifying identifier for the requested site is immediately activated whenever the computer establishes a connection. The request functions on the server using the patient's identifying context and is capable of carrying out any action that a legitimate user is capable of. The malicious webpage could: Run the computer code to start processing endlessly, in addition to pushing the post button. Send the data insight as a response from a Java applet. CSS was used to hide that box.

An image tag can be used to carry out an assault when it is targeted at Make destinations. This

type of assault is frequent on websites where JavaScript is prohibited but photos are permitted. Applications that modify resources or variables in response to GET responses are vulnerable to malicious attacks.

Violence committed at La - carte locations could be motivated by a visual element. On online forums that allow images but not JavaScript, this kind of violence is prevalent.

Malware can infect programs that change their state in response to Just Get requests, such as by altering parameters or assets.

The following chapter will go into greater detail about this subject and provide a thorough knowledge of the topic.

When creating a PHP online application, a web developer should consider security precautions. An unsecured online application is a prime target for hackers who want to steal sensitive information like credit and debit card numbers or client information. From this angle, a data leak may only have a peculiar impact on a person's company's operations and brand. PHP 1 implements the ten most effective security measures. Make regular updates to your PHP version.

Because security updates are frequently incorporated into subsequent versions, it's imperative to maintain an updated PHP version. Older PHP versions have known security flaws that hackers can exploit.

Your computer will crash unless you upgrade to some of the most recent standard calibrations.

A PHP beta version is also available for testing. The most recent version is 8.0.0 Beta 2. On the other hand, security professionals warn businesses against testing preview versions since security issues could still exist.

2. WATCH OUT FOR ASSAULTS ON SESSION MANAGEMENT (INTER-HACKING) RIGHT AWAY.

A buffer overflow attack, also known as multi-injection, occurs whenever any web software interacts with other data without human understanding. While your application is being processed, a cross-site scripting attack could occur; for instance, someone could enter any post that appears anywhere directly on a blog site. Remote ransomware should simply be launched if a bad consumer enters software, C++, or even new websites into their required format.

The code below displays a form that asks for input from users.

The aforementioned scripting element would produce a straightforward alert signal in the browsers. There seems to be a fixed condition here. From the other end, a hostile attacker might take a cookie or important confidential information. What exactly is the purpose of this then? Be careful to encapsulate sensitive user input to reduce backdoor and cross-site scripting attacks.

We shall examine the coming more closely inside. In the section that follows, you will learn about mirrored XSS attacks and how they impact our web application.

3. USE THE SQL STATEMENTS THAT WERE GENERATED.

Instantaneously applying input validation to an sq. statement is a typical mistake. This permits known vulnerabilities where the client can alter the SQL statement's original syntax and execute its variant.

For instance, the SQL statement in the query that follows uses unsterilized user data directly.

$users = MySQL query("SELECT * FROM `users` WHERE `id`='$ GET[id]'"); This allows a hacker to find a way around the statement and inquire for additional data, e.g. registrants' all information. A

SQL injection attack is consequently impossible because the entered data is escaped with a statement that is given.

Take note of the connect parameters method's first argument. The SQL statement will know what data you are feeding it thanks to this. The forename and surname parameters in this instance are both of the Text sorts. That additional security measure makes sure the incoming data type is correct. 4. Avoid putting the whole framework on your server.

Many PHP frameworks make use of the Model-View-Controller file structure. They have a sizable file structure as a result—the PHP Slim Framework. Let's look at the code, which is provided immediately below.

All of those things shouldn't be uploaded to your website's servers.

Only the relevant entries from either the accessible XHTML directory should be posted.

If you post all of your files to your server, malicious users will be able to examine your business logic. This helps them understand the software better and may enable them to take advantage of security holes or vulnerabilities.

5. CONSTANTLY VERIFY USER INPUT.

To ensure that an input order is written in an appropriate and considerate manner, the individual should always double-check the user information they have collected.

Many programmers utilize known values (regex) to validate file formats, such as birth date or cellphone number.

This code provides a simple definition of the history kept since a person's birth, taking the instance below into consideration.

ESTABLISH ORGANIZATIONAL CREDENTIALS IN STEP SIX.

You can restrict PHP's access to the information on the hard disk to make greater use of the allowed yield. The open premised method will only upload data into that subdirectory starting from the bottom if it is linked to the root of any program.

The allow-based approach would prevent a malicious attacker from reading sensitive information like /etc/password after gaining access to the website through PHP.

7. VERIFY YOUR SSL CONFIGURATIONS TWICE.

Each host has a TLS certification, enabling secure information exchange over SSL. Check your website frequently for outdated data encryption or weak cryptosystems.

Sysadmins frequently forget to update SSL certificates when they expire. On the other hand, an SSL certificate might help your website defend against XSS attacks.

USE URL ENCODING, PLEASE.

Creating proper URLs is made simple for programmers by PHP's urlencode function. According to the Mysql manual, the procedure is advantageous when putting a character into use in a population of this study that has a Web URL. Examine the situation below:

A URL is generated in response to a user request. In this specific scenario, a safe Address would be created using a URL encoding approach.

9. Avoid utilizing external files.

It is never a good idea to accept user input for a file need. The sample that follows shows a need statement with external files and user-generated content.

The viewer may have made a stupid error in the situation described above. the contents of the file that was supplied to the server will be displayed. Therefore, never make a page requirement based on user input. If you insist on opening a file that requires user input, make sure it is correct first.

Additionally, prevent directory access by using best practice number 6 using the open-based function. A switch statement could be a more effective method to specify the choices.

10. Bear in mind the importance of documentation.

Finally, make a record of everything you do. Keep track of any changes you make to your server, such as updating the browser and data system or changing the password, to ensure security.

When other developers need to modify the server in the future, they might find this information useful. People can quickly review recent occurrences thanks to it. In this manner, problems like a deprecated MySQL server password won't catch you off guard.

Additionally, documentation is a fantastic method for disseminating knowledge. If a developer leaves your company or becomes unwell, there is no knowledge loss. Documentation's primary objective is to transfer knowledge.

In the end, the user is responsible for both supplying the company's essential functionality and ensuring the code's integrity in their capacity as computer programmers.

The most important lesson from that blog is that input data should always be quintuple. Incorrect input data is a common source of security issues. Address security issues such as XSS attacks, URL encoding, and remote server injection. All of these problems are the result of incorrect user involvement.

MANAGEMENT OF PHP SESSIONS:

PHP tracks state using session management. Simply establish a session in a script that needs to maintain track of state, and utilize the $_SESSION variable to store information that can be accessed later.

Is that all, the whole story? I get what you're saying. "Is it accurate to say that only one variable is used to maintain sessions? What is a single variable's maximal power? "Single variables might retain all or most of the information in any program while yet allowing for an extension because variables are associative arrays that can carry an unlimited number of data storage (memory restrictions aside).

Consider this variable to represent a sizable chunk of designated memory space in multi-valued terms. These blocks can then carry other values, which in turn can hold more variables, and so on in an endless loop. PHP has an implicit array, which is a good feature, but these, like other variables, vanish when the script runs out of space. However, the $ Meeting parameter is on the opposite side. Whether viewers dismiss that tab or viewers direct them to stop, whichever occurs first, should remain in place. For language to be understood, it is used. Once the action is complete, the programming language stores this data in a cache to drive and restart the computer until the connection is no longer in use.

HERE IS AN ILLUSTRATION OF HOW THIS MIGHT BE PUT TO USE:

The script's line 3 calls the session start procedure (). Believe it or not, that is exactly what needs to be done when someone approaches enabling functionalities for HTML. After the session has begun, we can use the $_SESSION variable similarly to how we would use any other variable, with one significant exception: Everything that people set in place now after each program would be there now for the entire time the aforementioned or, in fact, many modules on that site that utilize cycle beginning is run ().

However, under these circumstances, one would prefer that his code continue to store inputs even if the client is restarted. The key option is enabled by a small modification shown in the following code. The session id () method allows us to give our session a name, and this property and code make it possible for someone to leave through the client's machine. The computer and data of the person handling the security issue will be impacted because it implies that the script is only being used to restore something that should not be lost at any cost. The system will be effectively protected using this strategy from all hackers and system attackers.

Would websites be able to save my info between computer starts while separating it from yours? shows how it might operate. You might also set a token on the internet device (lines 17–18) that saves their current session ID (line 15) as we begin our session variables. These cookies, for instance, have a 24-hour expiration date, but they free up enough space on your computer for us to retain their login information during that time. For security reasons, choose the website where all the information is accessible.

Information handling is made simple by the authentication method. Service disruption is far less likely to happen in a jumble of loose connections since the monitoring and reporting are received from that and saved on discs. The application can be accessed with the highest level of security possible today by utilizing HTTPS. Finally, technological innovation can help us reach a large audience while still enabling us to use some of its most potent web applications.

SESSIONS IN PH

When working with a program, you open it, make changes, and then close it. This is analogous to a Session. The computer can recognize you. When you use the program and when you don't, it can tell. On the internet, there is a problem: the website has no idea who or what you do because the HTTP address does not keep track of the state.

Sessions parameters address and resolve the problem by keeping user data that is applicable across other domains, such as a person's address and name, his hobbies, and regular employment. The connection characteristics are kept on file up until the reader closes the workstation. Sessions settings save information specific to a single user, making them accessible from all URLs within a single program.

ESTABLISH SESSIONS

Use the Meeting begin () function to start a client.

The briefing is a PHP property that stores temporary configurations.

To begin, create a unique organization called instance development of the website for PHP. In this book alone, we'll establish a brand-new PHP username and add a ton of new activity criteria.

We're going to make a new page named "example session2.php" right now. Following this tab, we can access the user information we created with the initial website ("demo session1.php").

User characteristics are not sent to each website individually; rather, they are automatically obtained from the actions users take at the beginning of each session (client establish()) or after each website (login end()).

Because of this, it's crucial to keep in mind that any temporary settings are preserved in the local $ Conversation attribute.

INPUT SESSION

Each of our datasets can be kept in the $ Meeting [] huge global collection as two keys. Throughout the sessions, it is possible to view the saved data whenever desired. Take a look at the software below, which adjusts two process parameters and creates a new account.

Use sessions begin () to re-establish the connection to get log data from all websites with the same website URL, and then fill out the $ Meeting array with the appropriate value.

Session destroyed

To remove certain backup data, simply use the appropriate $ Metadata arrangement component, as shown in the previous explanation.

To disconnect from a connection, simply use the sessions delete () function. This technique deletes all log data at once and requires no settings.

Each PHP connection has a delay value that indicates how long it must be active when no user data is received in terms of seconds. The

Meeting can have a different number. To adjust the computed maximum, simply use the go max lifetime option in the Html file name (PHP.iini).

ARE PHP SESSIONS SECURE?

The Multimedia Messaging System was created to start without a connection. This indicates that every request made to the server is complete and has all the information required for the server to provide the requested website. The connection's data or status are not tracked by the server. As a result, each communication that the supplier specifies for the customer can be handled separately.

Internet programs require a mechanism for keeping visitor context, from the ability to log identity management & grocery cart in commercial enterprises to longer information like prior purchases or discourse history in social media network programs.

This method may be improved or rewritten by inheriting the Session Holder class or implementing the Session Holder Interface.

PHP is built to save sessions as files only on the client. The config files stand in for the soon-to-go. PHP creates a PHPSESSEDSID cookie along with the client id whenever a transaction is started. The website only connects the token with the training data set once the visitor's machine performs a query, as is occasionally observed with such an experience. As a result, a web page's transactional data is retained across many websites.

In terms of security, PHP solutions outperform a solution that stores the software in passwords. The PHPSSSEESSID cookie contains a reference ID for an HTTP access file.

a Mysql system. It is acceptable to use technology to secure a location where temporary artifacts will be saved, as can be seen in PHP.big configuration files. It now can seriously weaken event credentials for additional clients. When one considers that possibly the bulk of Perl blogs are kept on common hardware with a small number of tenants, the situation becomes even more concerning. The most common session exploit is session hijacking.

When one considers that the bulk of Perl blogs is maintained on common hardware with so many tenants, the problem becomes even more concerning. WordPress's default selection for a location that can save transaction files is "/tmp," which can be found in php.ini system settings. The PHPSESSID cookie just carries a server reference ID. As a result, another user might seriously damage encounter data.

Once we learned that the bulk of scripting language blogs is hosted on network hosting with so many tenants, the situation become significantly more concerning.

Sessions Takeover is the account vulnerability that occurs the most frequently

PHP periods provide a higher level of security than a configuration where all programs are cached. a citation

The PHPSESSID cookie contains identification for a computer identity file.

CROSS-SITE SCRIPTING ATTACK (XSS)

Such a threat cannot be defended against at a meeting. The website must forbid the user's computer from processing any of their data. In general, any input data acquired by forms, GET variables, or other ways needs to be cleaned up before being used.

Typical web development network data that protects against vulnerabilities like these (e.g., SQL injection). htmlspecsdwialchars() and strip tags are two of the three most basic PHP text sanitization methods (). While htmlspecialchars() transforms special characters into web components, strip Tags() removes all HTML code, including the script> element. a unique session on metrics. A PHP.iini option is a cookie. HTTP oopaanly. Only this session, which is now well recognized as a fire networking system and has since been adopted by other browsers, was modified in the early days of working and performing work and complimented. It can be used to safeguard sensitive information.

IN-SESSION JACKING

This attack vector can be stopped by using SSL encryption spread over the entire request-response surface. The session cookie may still be compromised even if the connection is fully encrypted.

Self-consciousness, lack of assurance, unease, and precariousness not only lessen the security issue but also guarantee the strength of data accessibility and the problems related to it. The 303 coding topics are returned. The attacker would have been able to acquire and exploit the saved login information to compromise the user login, but the unlawful redirection route would have been sufficient to transmit it. How can the security of PHP user credentials be improved? There is a setting option in Word Press called "session." If you choose this option, you can use a password to get rid of this risk. When this option is selected, the browsers of the user are told to only send cookies via an HTTPS tunnel, and secure instructions are added to the Predefined something.

SETTING THE SESSION'S DATE

It is frequently used in Web address configuration files whenever an adversary tempts a user to use a predefined Session-Id. That means that the URL's login information is now included as only a GET parameter. One strategy is to use a hidden online form in an attacking player application to trick the target into thinking they need to sign up for anything. Passwords can be updated in several different ways to remedy a transaction. The Open Web Application Security Session has comprehensive information on Account Fixation concerns.

This security flaw's key PHP option would be used as a data transfer function, and data itself might be used. When set to 1, this parameter permits "invisible sessions," allowing PHP to send the session Token in hyperlinks if the user's identity isn't available. Transparent aminoglycosides have been deactivated out of an abundance of caution. If we configure our data according to the logic presented, it will experience (for instance, on a public computer) by searching the computer's cache for the URL containing the login Information or by looking at logs of intermediary companies. The session is another PHP substitute.

The only ones used (should be set to On by original) are cookies. Using URL elements as soon as they disappear is strictly forbidden with the same setting in place. Either of these variables needs to be set for session IDs to appear in URLs: One Sid is equal to one occurrence. utilizes a trans encounter Use only cookies=0.

FORECAST FOR THE SESSION

To avoid this entropy, web programs must produce Paramus that are sufficiently long and unpredictable. However, even though the standard PHP parameters in the most recent version of PHP (7.1.0+) are unquestionably safe enough, it would be crucial to keep that in mind if the software requires customized identity techniques. The PHP variables session can be used to change duration and unpredictableness.

Duration and activity of scud. lines with scud bits. This approach might be more practical and the session information will be more secure. The list of PHP session settings can be found here. This setting can be discovered in various information sources on coding, and coding can be very helpful for someone who uses it correctly.

CONCLUSION

To avoid this entropy, web browsers must create parameters that are sufficiently long and unpredictable. However, even though the standard PHP parameters in the most recent version of PHP (7.1.0+) are unquestionably safe enough, it would be crucial to keep that in mind if the software requires customized identity techniques.

The PHP variables session can be used to change duration and unpredictableness. Duration and activity of scud. lines with scud bits. The data we already have is very useful and secure in all provided materials, and the various parameters are useful in this section of all well-developed systems in the precise way of using data and understanding concepts of developing new systems. The information about each Meeting can be made secure and properly interpreted all by using the system, and the setting can be used with the help of our already present data. The Identifier unpredictability in Mysql reloading to v7.1.0 should be fine-tuned. You may get a detailed list of PHP session options here.

OPTIMUM PHP MANAGEMENT TECHNIQUES

Since its introduction in 1994, PHP has developed into both a framework for users to build dynamic web applications employing a server and a paradigm for database interaction.

Making static web pages more dynamic by performing logical operations in the server's backend and returning/outputting the results on the page, PHP is a very safe and efficient language that relies on the server, not the computer.

Any competent programmer at the very least is aware of the security concerns involved in creating websites and online apps. You knowingly make your code available to the general public, the world, and anyone who happens to pass by (good people and bad). One of PHP's early problems was putting user convenience ahead of code security (a quick Google search will turn up horror stories about relics like register global).

Thanks to improved, more secure defaults and deprecated functionality like register global, PHP is now safer than it has ever been online.

Even the most inexperienced web coders today seem to have a rudimentary awareness of security issues, even though the majority of security risks are produced by the programmer rather than the language.

Let's examine the top ten precautions that each website owner should do to secure their PHP website:

1. Protection for PHP sessions
2. Turn off the display of errors
3. There are limitations on file uploading.
4. Disable sensitive functions in PHP.
5. Disable Allow URL Open.
6. Magic quotations ought to be turned off.
7. Disable the register globes.

8. Trans Sid should not be used.

9. Use the appropriate php.ini file.

10. and examine PHP settings using "PhpSecInfo."

PHP SESSION SECURITY

Sensitive information is present on all dynamic websites and must be corrected to stop misuse due to session-related vulnerabilities.

YOU CAN DO THE FOLLOWING TO ENSURE THE SECURITY OF YOUR SESSION:

Use SSL while conducting crucial tasks or user authentication. (Visit sslforfree.com to obtain a free HTTPS certificate.)

Regenerate the session id whenever the security level changes (such as logging in). If you'd prefer, you may utilize the directive's regenerating session id option, which will automatically produce a new session id for each request.

SET A TIMER TO HALT SESSIONS AFTER A CERTAIN PERIOD.

The server should be used to store authentication credentials rather than utilizing the register globally. In other words, avoid including sensitive data in the cookie, like a login.

LOOK AT THE VARIABLE $_SERVER['HTTP USER AGENT'].

As a result, session hijacking encounters a small obstacle. Additionally, you may find someone's IP address. However, this creates problems for users that have a changing IP address due to, among other things, load balancing on several internet connections (which is the case in this context).

The proceedings should be closed to the public.

There are just two other noteworthy session attacks:

Attacks on the focus of the session.

By using session regenerate id, this is prevented ()

b) Taking Over a Session:

By using SSL Certificates to encrypt data, this might be prevented. Now, HTTPS will be used on your website instead of HTTP.

The phpinfo() function's replacement, phpSssecInfo, offers financial counsel and direction for enhancing the PHP environment. Although it doesn't perform any coding or software development, it can be a significant component of an all-encompassing security strategy.

MANUEL DE PHP

There are various formats in which the PHP manual is accessible. There are two different kinds of formats available: downloadable packages and online readable forms.

The manual can be found on some mirror sites as well as the PHP.net website. For optimum effects, select the nearest mirror. There are two HTML versions of the PHP manual available: plain (printfriendly) HTML and HTML which integrates the manual into the look and feel of the PHP website.

The incorporation of user notes and URL bookmarks, which may be used to rapidly access the pertinent guidebook chapters, are two elements of the online guide that set it apart from conventional paper editions. The problem of needing the internet to view this edition of the guidebook is evident.

The manual is available in a variety of forms that can be downloaded, with the appropriate platform depending on the Windows operating system and daily reading preferences. Check out the section of this supplement titled "Where we develop the included as" for more information on how the handbook is produced in its various iterations.

The most platform-independent version of the manual is the Xhtml version.

This is available as a single HTML document that can be downloaded or as a collection of smaller documents that may be used during various sessions. Sections for each section must always be handled carefully when dealing with other data. Therefore, to extract the files from the archives, you will need a decompression program.

The Microsoft HTML Help edition of the manual expands the XHTML format for use with desktop computers' Windows Hf Help software. This version has comprehensive indexing, pinning, and a thorough text search. Additionally, this type of data is accessible with ease thanks to several well-liked Microsoft PHP JavaScript frameworks. There are numerous Hcc viewers for Ubuntu computers. Look into it.

There is also an enhanced CHM version that has far more features but receives fewer updates. It will only run on Microsoft Windows due to the technology used to build the help pages.

A person improves his skills and has better thoughts about the system when he accesses a variety of knowledge sources. We may include reader feedback into the manual's primary text by allowing them to supply examples, suggestions, and further explanations directly from their browser. Additionally, the notes can be viewed in their provided form online and in a variety of offline formats until they are added.

In the manual, each function is described in depth for convenience.

Reading and comprehending the information will make learning PHP much simpler. Instead of relying on examples or cut-and-paste, everyone should be able to comprehend function definitions (prototypes). Let's start now:

Basic type knowledge is necessary. Despite PHP's poor typing, it is essential to understand the basics of types because of their importance.

The definition of a function specifies the kind of value that it will return.

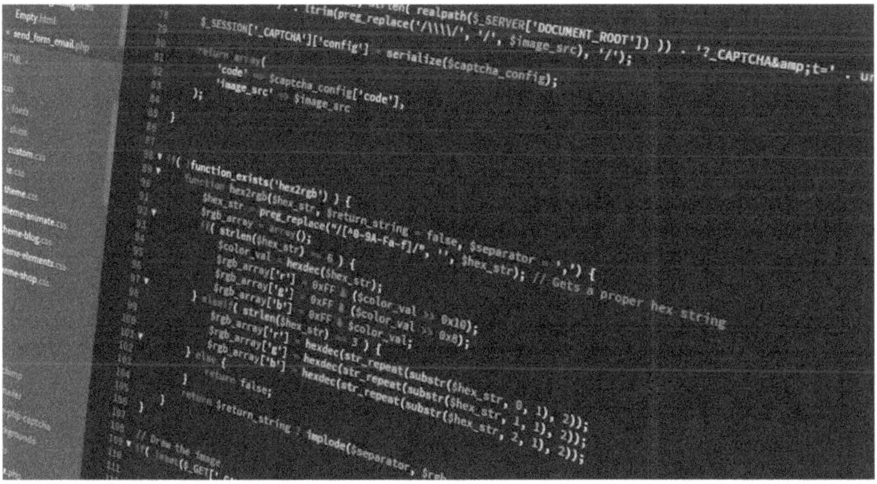

```php
            . ltrim(preg_replace('/\\\\/', '/', $_SERVER['DOCUMENT_ROOT'])) ) . '2_CAPTCHA&amp;t=' . ur
    $_SESSION['_CAPTCHA']['config'] = serialize($captcha_config);
    return array(
        'code'      => $captcha_config['code'],
        'image_src' => $image_src
    );
}


if( !function_exists('hex2rgb') ) {
    function hex2rgb($hex_str, $return_string = false, $separator = ',') {
        $hex_str = preg_replace("/[^0-9A-Fa-f]/", '', $hex_str); // Gets a proper hex string
        $rgb_array = array();
        if( strlen($hex_str) == 6 ) {
            $color_val = hexdec($hex_str);
            $rgb_array['r'] = 0xFF & ($color_val >> 0x10);
            $rgb_array['g'] = 0xFF & ($color_val >> 0x8);
            $rgb_array['b'] = 0xFF & $color_val;
        } elseif( strlen($hex_str) == 3 ) {
            $rgb_array['r'] = hexdec(str_repeat(substr($hex_str, 0, 1), 2));
            $rgb_array['g'] = hexdec(str_repeat(substr($hex_str, 1, 1), 2));
            $rgb_array['b'] = hexdec(str_repeat(substr($hex_str, 2, 1), 2));
        } else {
            return false;
        }
        return $return_string ? implode($separator, $rgb
    }
}

// Draw the image
if( isset($_GET[
```

Chapter 2

EXAMINE XSS AS A STARTER (SITE-TO-SITE SCRIPTING)

The harmful XSS variation that is placed into websites and web applications disrupt system operation, makes data accessible to hackers, and affects how the system of the end-user functions. Results may be impacted by using unclean or rejected Signals material in this procedure.

Some buffer overflow attacks don't use a single command to emphasize the significance; instead, they use a flaw in the website's programming. Any webpage that enters this system must be evaluated and used correctly throughout. This approach, in contrast, virtually always transfers data correctly and sequentially, which is critical for situations like sending an online message. A system flaw could make the social media application and the page development into a channel for spreading harmful mail to unaware clients' web browsers.

The code written in Visual Studio, Swf, Ole, and JavaScript, among many other languages, can be vulnerable to cyberattacks. Because it interacts with many of these clients often, XSS frequently targets JavaScript. XSS attacks are dangerous and common in that they can take advantage of regularly used systems.

HOW TO USE A CROSS-SITE SCRIPTING

We now know what a threat like that posed by past programming is; nevertheless, to fully comprehend it, we must examine how it operates.

Consider the circumstance of a person using a laptop while sitting down.

In the lower-right corner of the screen, there are icons for a file explorer, word processor, calculator, and audio player program. So far, everything has gone as expected. However, this picture is lacking one important component. an internet browser that has numerous pages open at once. These sections provide exciting news, humorous videos, commercials for tangible products, links to online stores, and a website for transactions that have already processed a reimbursement for a traffic ticket.

These web pages all share one thing in common: they couldn't exist without JavaScript. Customers will only be directed to a different domain by clicking on either of the two advertisement posters. A piece of malware on that website connects to a mobile gaming system and secretly sends money from the victim's computer to their

MasterCard. Keeping with the analogy They do not believe that is a wise decision. This policy forbids web page scripts from accessing private data. The browser won't be able to run scripts loaded from another domain.

VIRUS-RELATED WEBSITE INFECTION

As our system is improved, JavaScript from many related types of things may cause this issue. Analyzing the same kind of data and system-based work that is utilized for reading is hindered by the same restriction. Even the website hosting the browsing page is not now under the control of the hackers. Now, it's odd how they gain access even if they can't do so directly; this is tricky and needs to be further investigated. Let's examine how this all works and what makes it possible for hackers to insert pieces of potentially hazardous software into internet content, which can help attackers and increase risk.

Some common search engines, for instance, duplicate the user inputs when the user enters a search query.

Perhaps if a user types "<script alert (1) /script>" into the search box? Will the details on the search results page trigger this function, resulting in the appearance of a discussion box with the number "1"? This depends on web app programmers' ability to effectively check user input. The crux of the issue is that customers are employing broad categories of programming that can be comprehended for this purpose and are leveraging data.

Each browser approaches interacting with internet pages in a somewhat different way. The Efficient operation may occasionally be incredibly effective when sources are still not sufficiently filtered. The first step in using data very securely and attempting to avoid any corrupt system that can crash the device is deciding whether to launch an Attack vector.

A website that is infected is used to attack the systems.

The attacker will then attempt to convince the victim to visit a specific website. The website should also get the vulnerabilities from the adversary. There is no significant obstacle at all in this section. A URL is consistently thought of as including data. A variety of social engineering or luring tactics can be used by attackers to exploit all system weaknesses.

The additional code that follows in the customer's response exemplifies such a string (provided by the customer in the HTTP protocol) perfectly.

The program inspects all of the data in the second HTTP element of the client. After that, the property is displayed on the newly created website page. The programmer seemed to be expecting only text data without any HTML elements for the first Name selection.

You may verify that the program indicated in the first Identified URL argument is performed once this XML snippet has been added to a brand-new website on the web server. In this instance, the vulnerable website's exposed portion runs risky Java. As a result, the website's HTTP and other features may be viewed by your scripts.

Naturally, the perpetrator will fabricate the real route to hide their existence on the client's website.

THREATS FROM (XSS) CAN TAKE MANY DIFFERENT FORMS.

Cross-site scripting (XSS) attacks typically fall into one of three categories:

It became apparent (unsteady). The attacking dynamic array carrier is the current customer Web service. The server's response must include the threat channel. In a sense, the computer replicates the assault.

collectibles and antiques (persistent). The approach pathway is established on the server side. (We will discuss how it got there in a later section of this article.)

One variety of XSS is evidenced in XSS (Document Object Model).

The assault is aimed at the client. Due to flaws in the data collecting code of JavaScript, the system is accessible.

Below are a few additional categories. Although they are not as frequent as the preceding ones, they are nevertheless a component of the procedure, the details of which are as follows:

The foundation of XSS is light. The root of the problem is poor user-provided management among Macromedia developers.]

XSSI (Extensible Stylesheet Specification Interface).

Other names and computers are used to store unsecured materials.

Computer bugs could potentially make client-side risks worse, including • uXSS (Universal XSS). It is possible to go around the SOP and run Js via the fault from one domain to another.

Multi XSS (mXSS) (Mutation XSS). Intruders insert a Markup payload into the HTML using "JavaScript ([element].innerHTML = cost is enormously% " or "document.write (consumers are highly%)" to change this from acceptable to extremely destructive.

Mirrored XSS; it doesn't last yet it mirrors

In mirrored XSS, the attack technique is covered by the demands of Internet users, which are either handled by the client or the client itself. If the demand or response is thematically linked, the device's response is determined from the dataset or the data retrieved. A search word may be entered, the data may be in the form of an illustration, and the result may have been a results page.

Every time the node misinterprets HTML escape sequences, evidenced XSS happens. In this scenario, the backend page—which would be half of the first infected machine—would enable Java to operate there in the server context. An illustration of a mirrored (quasi) XSS

Here is an example of software that is (XSS)-vulnerable:

XSS THAT IS PERMANENTLY STORED

This kind of readiness evaluation takes place when a threat uses PHP that is not a component of something else, like client requests. The programming is once more first obtained from the internet using a similar online database.

You might be able to use the program to save data from an anonymous narrator and then use that data to create an HTTP request in response to a patient's request. As a result of this and the inadequate handling of XML escaped characters, a stored Attack is typically plausible.

Imagine a community online where members communicate regularly. If the program is weak, an enemy could send HTML-containing signal materials. The DBMS will retain the comment. After that, any users who read the shooter's email will be blocked.

Here is an example script that can be used to attack hidden security flaws:

Instead of being Dbl, reading and writing data from a source and sending it to the browser. The content will only be exposed to clients and used by the viewer inside this web app if the information data contain Xhtml enclosing elements, such as Flash.

assaults on the DOM

The problem is the same for both types of Url flaws: the client-side creation of the web URL with concealed HTML.

On the other hand, shareholder libraries are frequently used in historical online programs to start editing a website without traveling to the servers. The content object reference type may be easily changed here on the client side.

The fundamental idea driving all of this trouble is still the same: badly coded Xhtml escape sequences decoding.

Therefore, the internet column's content contains the opposing Jquery. This action is then carried out from the viewpoint of a passenger.

Threats, in contrast, rely solely on HTML documents (DOM).

The "communication" attribute in HTML and JavaScript refers to a container that shows the words of a text. With additional verification and an adequate understanding of the issue, the DOM hierarchy is created appropriately.

The HTML () technique, which does not sanitize HTML escaped characters, is used to display the statement. Because of this, a structure like this is weak. For instance, the data may be provided for the following feature:

code ("XSS") alert> script ("XSS") warning> PHP ("XSS") warn> code ("XSS") Code>

The application will be run in this scenario from the viewpoint of the client.

CROSS-SITE SCRIPTING EXAMPLES (XSS)

There is something to bear in mind when we look at specific occurrences. Some XSS attacks are meant to only gather information once.

On occasion, malicious software is downloaded onto the victim's computer, sending stolen data to a website under the control of the attacker.

On the other side, these assaults aim to exploit flaws in gaining control over a user's behavior and entering the accounts to collect data

using fraudulent login information to access such a facility.

Change the passwords used by the offender forever. If the application enables users to access or alter your account before ever entering the prior account (or a one-time code), then this is possible.

As a result, the attacker can create a new, strong identity while it appears that they have the authority to use it.

Please be aware that the attacker must be able to modify site content to create a gateway using Query. Cached Cross-site on frequently visited URLs may be provided if the user has adequate access. Cross-site scripting implementations have been targeted by application assaults leveraging the Facebook WordPress dashboard's blueprint publisher or Mambo game attacks that take advantage of the victims' abilities.

frequency reduction brought about by an unexpected upgrade As we've seen, spoofing allows

Python to continue to execute on the same victim system. Scripting, but Password, naturally occurring, Asap, or other markup languages, function in both the typical consumer's search engine and the

Google search engine. The primary goal of a cross-site explosion should be to gain access to the child's information. The information and objects provided describe the procedure through which it operates.

HIJACKING

Think about the scenario below. In this illustration, a web system is used to access a website for online banking. A device's passcode must always be entered to log in. Without a doubt, consumer behavior must be regarded as legal. But how can their validity be confirmed if the visitor cannot sign in before each link is examined?

Fortunately, customers can do this in a certain way. Following the system logging in, each provider provides a message to identify the current consumer transaction. The password material used in the design is given as an integer. assuming the persona of someone similar to the current consumer.

This programming language operates with a great deal of capacity and is quite professional and accurate. In a highly secure and appropriate system, an attacker can utilize these skills in conjunction with cross-site scripting vulnerabilities. Instead of just collecting private user information, this application can be used to safeguard against weak systems and programming languages.

For accurate feedback and an accurate understanding of all problems, utilize the coding provided below. The website creates appropriate terminology and software to use new data queries. The code provided below can fix the aforementioned issues because they are automatic and frequently go unnoticed. These questions can be used to get feedback.

Foreign opponents can utilize these software flaws and deposit any amount of money into bank accounts by using an unauthorized person.

PONZI SCHEMES

As previously mentioned, JavaScript applications that modify the DOM model can be inserted into a web page using XSS. This gives a perpetrator the ability to add a fake textbox and change how the webpage appears to the viewer. A hacker could use the underlying security flaws to put fake login information into such a blog site if a vulnerable application process aids Xhtml prototype modifications. The outcomes could be extremely risky and unethical.

These attack samples and attack pathways demonstrate how important it is for an attacker to make an effective SQL injection attempt on a compromised employment website.

Adversaries may exploit occurrences to carry out the following:

You can read any data and carry out any actions by imitating the user. Such behaviors include things like making social media posts and paying bills.

Recognize and block human input.

WEBSITES ARE VANDALIZED.

Online sites have malicious code inserted onto them. You might be reminded of Trojans by such characteristics, such as fake forms for inputting login information or making payments for online orders.

Sending money through this website's technique can be quite complicated and risky because it is very vulnerable to hacking. Severe XSS attacks can be quite harmful to the system, and we can suppose that the system's effects could be utilized to include commercial content or change Internet ratings by manipulating the DOM.

AMOUNTS OF XSS VULNERABILITIES AT RISK

Analyze the difficulty of a SQL intravenous infusion strategy, including how difficult it is to use it, how difficult it is to store or show, and whether validation is required given that everyone has accessed the system.

Considerations include whether the user needs to do any additional actions, from the user's perspective, what exactly needs to be done before transferring any data, and what exactly a possible attacker stands to gain. If the site does not contain personal information, the impact is minimal; the data supplied to the user must be safe and beneficial.

According to Positive Technologies' Security Threatscape, there are three categories for the early stages of data use and sharing:

Low: Vulnerabilities in routers or other local devices that demand authorization. In this situation, privileged user rights are required for XSS, or to put it another way, self-XSS. The impact is negligible because an attack's difficulty is relatively high.

Medium: The majority of forecasted archived Dos assaults that demand that a user browse a specific website's daily data use are found in this section. It is even more crucial but has a greater impact when offenders can frequently abuse stored Deadlocks. As a result, this intensity is now less severe because the client must participate at first.

High: In this instance, the visitor sees a page with a risky script on it. Other possible instances in the directory listing that uses a password or in records that use an authenticator include user input for a personalized touch, posting comments, and maybe website upkeep that happens right away.

There's a chance that XSS was left on a website, which would have a significant impact. The impact is now just Medium; when a user needs to log in using their ID, he or she must be particularly knowledgeable about the privacy regulations of websites.

It's also important to remember that the author's evaluation of the criticality determines the impact in any case. There are three different angles of view for each investigator. Although

Metasploit weaknesses can be exceedingly hazardous, they often receive higher scores than comparable assaults. Testing and XSS detection.

The quickest approach to verifying native software or one for requirements they currently have software appears to be the combination of manually checking and input validation methodologies. A code quality analysis should help to stop several XSS vulnerabilities. The scanner significantly affects how accurately things are found. Since no scanner is perfect, some may be more reliable than others because they use different vectors and methods. In contrast, a human inspector might be able to spot issues that even a dark-skinned scanner would miss.

Someone might build a grey-box/white-box alternative to support the mixed-race technique and boost unit testing penetration.

It's also important to take into account the potential for false-positive outcomes. Although combining strategies and technologies will increase productivity, some problems might still need to be identified manually.

Every security detector for buffer overflows requires Js and XML data. If the decoder could identify the Code generator in any area of something like the screen, it would never be properly communicated to the analyst. This suggests that a Buffer overflow attempt could be made while deceiving the translator and entirely evading the analyzer.

The list of programs that the Apricot analyzer doesn't in some way recognize at the time the documentary is shown is provided below.

INJECTION OF FUNCTION:

Our software had trouble identifying any potential XSS vulnerabilities in the script, including in both circumstances. If you understand what you're trying to do, you can infer that the testing step is by far the most effective method.

Testing outside of a comment section is an alternative. It is challenging to stay error-free. If people insert JavaScript, examine the generated webpage, and then watch precisely what happens when the variable is changed, you will undoubtedly find it.

You may cover a wide range of potential attack vectors by employing a similar approach:

1. Seek out locations without any further character filtering (>" "). Burp Suite or Acunetix can automate this procedure. After automatic verification, confirm that any manually entered text has been filtered. The next step is to look over the JavaScript code for the project. Your complete front end may be properly tested using Blue Closure. Observe how the software displays to the user or how it is transmitted toward the network saved on the database and coding system after you have fixed any automatic vulnerabilities.

Next, take the entire platform—possibly excluding the HTML software. For instance, some components convert user input into backlinks and other navigational elements. A cyberattack circuit is created by placing a link like "Typescript: notice (1)" in a client comment's webpage column. Every decoder that converts language to Web pages has the potential to inject malware.

START TAKING THE FOLLOWING FACTORS INTO ACCOUNT:

- Users can add custom HTML content to their forum posts using markdown editors (including harmful JavaScript).
- Text-to-emoji and text-to-link email converters that can be tricked into creating a URL for an infected element.
- the transformation of images into the content.

XSS ATTACK PREVENTION AND MITIGATION

An injection problem called XSS occurs when a hacker tampers with the semantics of a computer program. Every piece of external data that enters the system could be thoroughly reviewed to reduce errors. The software will use several tactics to do this, which we will go through in more detail in the preceding context.

the application of related data types.

The customer's donation is initially displayed as a sentence. This data has to be translated into a certain type of unit.

Even though this functionality is offered at the associated duties, most visitors are ignorant of it. The code that is written below shows one thorough system:

Foreign opponents can utilize these software flaws and deposit any amount of money into bank accounts by using an unauthorized person.

PONZI SCHEMES

As previously mentioned, JavaScript applications that modify the DOM model can be inserted into a web page using XSS. This gives a perpetrator the ability to add a fake textbox and change how the webpage appears to the viewer. A hacker could use the underlying security flaws to put fake login information into such a blog site if a vulnerable application process aids Xhtml prototype modifications. The outcomes could be extremely risky and unethical.

The code provided above provides information on how to prevent data loss. This can be accessed by using the relative path "/result," and its two required inputs are an integer scan-id and a word artifact. The foundation then performs the steps required to assess the accuracy of the data during the preliminary treatment.

Upon viewing the program code, the enquiring group receives an explanation notice if there is even one class problem. This might happen if the analyzer's argument contains what appears to be a quasi-integer or an example.

VERIFICATION OF DATA

Before data evaluation, data must be verified and examined after being entered into the system. The user's year of birth can be checked for grammar using the regular phrase "[0-9]4$". The string has exactly four (and only four) digits; after transforming the input, one can check the syntax when converting a number to an integer; this equation states that the year of origin should not be excessive.

During checking, permission listings and spam filters can be helpful. If you're trying to find something akin to a shortlist, you need to provide specific patterns that shouldn't be found in the incoming data.

Contrarily, blocklist approaches have several significant disadvantages. Patterns frequently involve unnecessary complexity and age quickly. Finding patterns that cover all conceivable incarnations of dangerous data is difficult. Once hackers access the data, it will eventually be more difficult to get past things. The main justification for this was the efficiency of employing an allow list, which establishes requirements for input data to meet.

CLEANING OF THE OUTPUT

The transfer of data from the local approach to the vital level of the data is the most important phase in the process of prevention, regardless of how well (or poorly) the previous two solutions are accomplished. All of the data must be secure and dependable to avoid data from being shared and decreased to provide an HTML document with unreliable data. There are a few exceptions, including when data must still abide by particular regulations. The main instructions must be carefully followed and comprehended; otherwise, we can only guarantee that shared

data is secure and inaccessible to hackers.

ADDITIONAL XSS PROTECTIONS

The additional information is used to regulate the data and appropriately assess it; it is the most common but not the only method. One must examine the applied code again after discovering the problem in the data.

- • Messaging and Cross should be coordinated at the top corner element. Hypertext markup language should be used as an alternative to the uptime genre if it turns out to be plain "but also that the text box a user is using might be abused and that the machine does not always recognize it Cin: none puff.

- • Hackers have a history of inserting hazardous codes into data, which is incredibly risky for the information being shared and shouldn't be done so casually.

- Prevent simple data leaks.

- You can steer clear of a variety of XSS attack vectors with the help of this cheat sheet. Even basic suggestions will stop the majority of attackers. The following are the most crucial:

- • Until the information is relocated to a secure location, access will only be denied.

- • Use CSS scrambling while adding unauthorized users inside an XHTML frame.

- • When allowing unauthorized users to encode fundamental attributes, perform web page aspect scrambling.

- • Remove Jquery before adding suspect input to the supplied data. • Constantly isolate Stylesheet for entering inaccurate data into the Web page's decorative land values.

- • Encrypt Addresses after inserting harmful files in CSS Http attribute values.

- • Have been extracting and cleaning Encoding tuples using a package. Even if there may be risks associated with consumers using a service that has vulnerabilities, it is crucial to consider privacy from a variety of perspectives. Engineers must be informed of proper code and detailed recommendations.

checks the codes as regularly and quickly as possible to look for errors and breaches. Visitors with administrator rights or the capacity to change a webpage should receive extra attention. To have a deeper understanding of web hosting, look at reliable websites like the Jboss Note Card.

PT AI'S XSS TESTING TOOL

XSS is an injection problem in which the input (which comprises the attack surface) may lead to the logic of potentially harmful functionality changing. Instrumental analysis The utilization of codebase is one of the best detecting techniques. A solution that uses several novel ways to find flaws in current applications is the promising Data Service Inspectorate (PT AI).

Pb AI identifies vulnerabilities and develops assaults to test them. Additionally, it enables you to assess research data realistically because of the graphical flow charts that show how a problem could be solved.

The accompanying key differentiator's data flow diagram is a crucial element of any computer system that needs to be thoroughly understood. The Pure Java client of the traditional editor reproduces it.

HERE ARE A FEW INSTANCES:

1. At the taint entry point, the request's NAME parameter value is read.

Returning the response in HTML with a potentially dangerous function involves data processing.

Infusion attacks, also known as merge script authoring, involve pushing unwanted software into often respectable and innocent domains (SQL injections). When an attacker uses an online system to spread a computer virus to another user, typically through an Internet Explorer side script, this is called Metasploit. Because a website properly verifies or encrypts user information before displaying it, it may be possible to detect the faults that allowed these processes to run.

Players can take advantage of XSS to send javascript code to a user who is unaware of the vulnerability. The internet user who is similar to the person has no way of understanding that the function should not be taken into consideration but will still be available. Because that would imply that it wrote the movie.

Chapter 3

HIJACKING A SESSION

What does "session hijacking" refer to? A spoofing assault occurs when an adversary seizes control of a web cycle, except when someone affects a person's visa billing statement, processes payments, or conducts online comparison shopping. The two platforms that identity thieves most frequently target are Safari and open application engagements. Following that, a node capture hacker has access to the website and is free to do anything they choose. A hijacker tricks the website into believing they are you.

Similar to how an airplane can be hijacked and its occupants put in danger, a session hijacking can take over a session and pose serious issues for the user.

How did session hijacking develop its practical value and fundamental operational protocols?

Below, we will discuss each of the many types of session hijacking attacks in detail and with examples. But initially, upcoming topics will outline the hijacking's operating premise and importance.

Initial session hijacking protocol: A clueless online user subscribes to a service. The user may access a bank balance, a website for credit or debit cards, an online market, or another app or website. The app or website provides a brief overview of the subject, which is more helpful for comprehending the actual issue. This cookie preserves the user's information, allowing the website to keep them authorized and signed in while also keeping track of their activities. The session cookie is kept in the browser until the users check out, at which point the browser logs them out for them.

Taking over a session Step 2: Use a variety of techniques when the hackers try to assault the user's website and the individual pauses to grasp the fundamentals. Stealing is a part of session hijacking. When an enemy takes control of any online cycle, especially when someone is seeking to influence the other's immigration proforma invoice, paying bills, or comparison shopping, a faking foreground of this change is present. Identity thieves commonly prey on Game drives and unprotected website interfaces.

Taking over a session The next step involves paying the session hijacker for the time they stole. Once the original web user has exited the session, the hijacker can utilize it to carry out a variety of damaging actions.

terrorists may close a sale, obtain personal information to complete a fraud, extort money from a recipient's direct deposit, encrypt private information, and demand payment.

So, the following are some scenarios in which a login may be compromised:

Example No. 1 Bridget is sipping on a mocha and checking her investment balance in a coffee shop. To steal the tracking cookies, take control of the system, and have the authority to take goods from a person's account, a thief uses "session sniffing" at the adjacent table; it is very difficult to acquire the cookies back after that.

When Jeremy gets a letter announcing a sale at his preferred online store, he signs on and starts shopping. The attacker made a point of focusing on the URL in the message, which was crucial. The opponent retakes control of the transaction and proceeds to commit a series of crimes using Liam's previously saved payment method.

Process pirates use a variety of tactics to capture experiences, so it's important to know exactly what works so you can stay secure offline.

Five: Are you familiar with the hijacking process?

Would you like to learn more about session hijacking? Understanding how hijacking operates and the various types of hijacking—which are listed below—is crucial.

1. External source: The hacker obtains the transaction password and uses it to his advantage in an attack to seize the transaction. Brute force attacks work best when a site's defenses are weak and the session keys are quick and easy to guess.
2. A sort of attack known as cross-site scripting (XSS) makes use of security holes in a web server. To introduce software into

websites, an attacker employs cross-site scripting. Your computer will run more slowly and improperly as a result of these problems.

3. Malware: To steal a transaction, scammers can trick clients into clicking a link that downloads malware or viruses. The virus could use research and "conversation probing" to identify a period. Your login information is then taken by the malware and given to the offender, who may use it to steal your login information and take over your computer's identity.

4. Session side jacking: This is done when hackers obtain a person's personal information and that information leads to a dangerous location.

The user may acquire access if they utilize man-in-the-middle attacks or connect to an unsecured Wi-Fi network. These assaults could cause the user to lose their data permanently and have highly hazardous repercussions. 5. Session correction: In a transaction obsession attack, the perpetrator establishes login information and induces the victim to utilize it to start a session. One typical method of doing this is by emailing the customer a link to the registration page for the company the offender wants to visit. Since the user logs in using a fake session ID, the attacker can get permission.

The following side-channel strategies were among the most common. As you can see, the majority of spoofing techniques either assume or collect tracking cookies that are already in place or trick the client into checking in using the shooter's specific Id.

1. LET'S EXAMINE IT MORE CLOSELY.

Using trial-and-error, brute force, also known as a brute force attack, is a technique for breaking encryption keys, login credentials, and passwords. It is a straightforward but efficient technique for gaining unauthorized access to both individual accounts and the networks and systems of companies.

The hacker tries multiple usernames and passwords until they find the correct login information, typically using a computer to test a wide range of combinations.

Insecure attackers that use excessive force to enter user accounts are referred to as having "brute strength." Although brute force is a well-established hacking method, hackers continue to employ it since it has been tried and tested.

THE VARIOUS BRUTE FORCE ATTACK TYPES

Several brute force attack strategies may be used by attackers to obtain unauthorized access and steal data from users.

1. COMMON ATTACKS

Because of their expertise, hackers that attempt to access our username and password without using any software are doing so. It is common practice to utilize conventional password combinations or personal identification number (PIN) codes.

Information is processed from one computer to another computer since so many users always utilize online accounts or other online activities.

Other than looking up people's favorite basketball club crest, predators could also find usernames by conducting some preliminary study on a potential secret.

2. INSULTS TO THE DICTIONARY

The attacker chooses a subject and links usernames to the client's identity in a thesaurus attack that mercilessly penetrates security. The assault approach could help a public figure uncover a secret even though it's not nearly a nasty tactic. Dictionary assault is a concept that has gained popularity because of attackers who have searched vocabularies and changed words with unique digits. This form of defense is often ephemeral and appears to have a low probability of success when compared to new, increasingly effective attack strategies.

the back-affecting attacks.

To launch a backward attacker's attack, a malicious user must have a breached password, which is again typically discovered as a result of a networking attack. Numerous subscribers are screened for a login identification that matches that password. Hackers may attempt to find a match in a user database by using a widely used strong password, such as "Password123," as a starting point. When an attacker submits numerous usernames or alphanumeric passwords in an attempt to properly guess each one, it is known as a frightening attack in the field of cryptography.

Until the right one is found, the adversary keeps examining all default settings and cryptographic operations. If this doesn't work, the criminal will come up with a plan to estimate the key, which is often obtained from either the message or a decryption function. Searching for vital capacities is what this is known as.

A user launches a backward conventional warfare assault by using a prior passcode they discovered from a network heist. They are sifting through hundreds of identities for a connection using that account.

Additionally, a hacker may check a database of identities for connections using a widely used unique password A force of nature attack on cybersecurity involves entering a vast number of combinations or cryptographic operations in the hopes of accurately guessing them all. Until the right one is found, the adversary continually attempts all default combinations and cryptographic functions. If not, the attacker will come up with a plan to estimate the key, which is often obtained from the text using a decryption function.

THIS IS REFERRED TO AS THOROUGH KEY SEARCHING.

By misrepresenting the information to be delivered, making it more difficult for the intruder to detect when encryption has been broken or making the attacker work hard to prove an assumption, force of nature attacks are given a tremendous boost. One gauge of its durability has been the amount of time needed for an opponent to successfully conduct a force of nature operation against such a secret Latin alphabet.

3. HYBRID BRUTE-FORCE ATTACKS

A thesaurus attack force combined with a straightforward conventional warfare assault is referred to as a combination network incursion. It all starts with a thief getting a user, then using that user's password and standard warfare techniques to find an online bank number. The hacker starts with a list of alphabetic characters before attempting several symbols, paragraphs, and alphanumeric characters to obtain the right credentials. By combining common or rare terms with integers, seasons, or random characters, identities like "Sibersdho12223" or "Roorr2111," which combine these elements, can be found.

4. FALSIFYING DOCUMENTS

Taking advantage of people's bad passphrase habits is ethical hacking. Hackers collect stolen login credentials and try them on different websites to see if they can access more user profiles. This tactic can be used by clients that utilize the same screen name combination across many websites and online forums.

WHAT MAY A METHOD BASED ON NATURAL FORCES ACHIEVE?

Attack hacking requires a lot of restraint because it can take a year to crack a password or decryption code. The benefits are tremendous on both ends.

MAKE GOOD USE OF ACTIVITY DATA OR ADVERTS.

A hacker might use brute force against a website or a collection of websites to make money off of advertising commissions. Here are a few illustrations of typical methods:

1. By posting spam advertisements on well-known websites, the attacker can get money each time a user clicks or views an advertisement.
2. It's against the law to steer traffic from an authorized website to a paid-for advertisement site.
3. Using spyware or another type of tracking software to infect a website and its users. Without the user's awareness or consent, the collected data is then sold to marketers.
4. Getting Individual Information

Theft of a participant's finances may disclose a wealth of information, including personal patient histories, financial information, and account numbers. When a hacker gains access to a customer's computer, they may impersonate them, take their property, sell their credentials to other people, or utilize the information to carry out more complex operations. Sensitive data and login credentials may be lost as a result of business data compromise, in which thieves get access to a key piece of corporate data.

Malware is proliferating.

The overwhelming majority of the attacks are not targeting a particular person. An attacker might simply want to wreak havoc and show off its nefarious prowess. They might accomplish this by using email to distribute software, hiding spyware on a different phone homepage, or directing blog readers to dangerous websites.

By infecting a participant's workstation with spyware, the attacker can gain access to linked machines and apps and conduct larger attacks that target organizations.

nefarious behavior Hijacking Mechanisms

Unsavory individuals can utilize attacks to build larger network attacks with a variety of devices.

A distributed cognitive dissonance (Intrusion detection system (ids) assault is frequently used to overwhelm the attacker's defenses and skills.

THE REPUTATION OF A BUSINESS OR WEBSITE MIGHT BE HARMED.

Companies are regularly exposed to conventional military assaults in a plot to seize information, which already makes them rich but also affects their prestige. Publications may contain offensive text or images, ruining the reputation of the company and maybe leading to termination.

TOOLS FOR BRUTE-FORCE ATTACKS

It can take a while to predict a participant's social networking page username, especially if the questions are challenging.

To make the task of improving security simpler, thieves have developed tools and software. Attackers and pin code tools can break passcode combinations that are nearly hard for a human to figure out on their own.

Examples of tools used frequently in conventional warfare include the following: A group of techniques known as music streaming can be used to hack a corporation by impersonating base stations and sending false signals, as well as to monitor and transmit statistics and analyze the connectivity of local area networks

.In addition to recovering passwords for Windows, Ubuntu, and Macintosh, data warehouses, online services, internet traffic, encoded authentication tokens, and document files utilizing thousands of encryption and pattern variants, Jack the Pulverize is an intelligible username password tool. Some programmers can break into a range of technical devices, including cellular phones and secured memory sticks, by swiftly assuming credential sequences. A substantial number of cups may be required for a conventional military assault.

Developers have created new architectural strategies to deal with this, such as fusing a smartphone's microprocessor with graphics chips (GPU). To make pin code cracking considerably easier and quicker for cybercriminals, the CPU data processing power unit was introduced. This allowed the programmer to manage numerous projects one at a time.

In what ways are brute force attacks preventable?

Some of the greatest methods for coming up with a stronger password include the ones listed below:

1. Make effective, non-username, and non-linear usernames: Passcodes should, as a rule of thumb, be between five and ten paragraphs long and contain capital letters, groupings of letters, punctuation, and numerals. The time it takes to crack a secret increases significantly, from a few minutes to several millennia, unless the attacker has access to a microprocessor.

2. Make your usernames more difficult: While adding extra letters to personal usernames is a sensible move, many businesses have username strength restrictions. Use complex usernames as a corollary to protect yourself from straightforward phishing attacks. Passing is a group of letters or portions that have distinctive marks that make choosing more challenging.

3. Establish authentication standards: reducing the length of words to make them appear absurd to people who read these is yet another original passcode technique. This is done by eliminating syllables or using only the first main individual of

utterances, then creating a punishment for the incomplete utterances. Blue is abbreviated to "bl," whereas "hope" is represented as "hp."

4. Avoid using already-used usernames. Frequently used encryption keys, such as a nickname, an athletic league, or even a "password," are especially risky. nefarious intentions for common feelings and phrases in people's credentials and strategies to enter organizations using these terms.

5. Make passphrases for each of the following: Cybercriminals that practice ethical hacking verifies usernames that have previously been on networks to determine whether they have previously spent money on other things. Unfortunately, it is a tremendous success since people frequently reuse their identities for personal conversations, social networking sites, and online publications. It's important to avoid using the same login for a lot of different websites or organizations.

6. Individuals can easily create secure passphrases for each service they use by using online services. It generates and keeps track of users' online accounts on several hosts that contain all of your login information by using secure passwords. Users can create lengthy, difficult credentials with the use of a passcode.

IMPROVED USER PASSWORD PROTECTION

If a user's employer cannot protect their data from brute force attacks, there is little purpose in encouraging them to use strong passwords.

The business must also take measures to safeguard its users and improve network security, like:

1. Accept Verification Usernames and Passwords: An attacker is stopped from brute-forcing her route into a username or a network by providing a Riddle window in the account creation. Examples of Scrambler alternatives include typing words into on-screen visuals, checking various image squares, and detecting objects.

2. Purchase an IP filter to protect your internal network and staff from current criminals: An IP whitelist is a wise choice for protecting a company's infrastructure, including its customers, from known intruders. To prevent future attacks, it is essential to keep this whitelist updated.

WHAT DOES "ENCRYPTION KEY" ACTUALLY MEAN?

Personal information encryption is a technique for mumbling issues into an odd assortment of individuals. The proper security password will allow you to decipher the material. A 256-bit encryption method would require two to the power of 128 possibilities to decode, which is only generally possible on super supercomputers. Nearly all websites and online browsers make use of it. Even a supercomputer that can analyze billions of possibilities per second wouldn't be able to break the data protection used by 256-bit encryption. Therefore, 256-bit encryption cannot be cracked by brute force methods.

WHAT CAN FORTINET DO TO HELP?

FortiNet's FortiWeb web application firewall shields businesses from brute force attacks (WAF). Mission-critical online applications are shielded by FortiWeb against sophisticated attacks that make use of both known vulnerabilities and zero-day exploits. The system adapts to the rapidly evolving security environment, ensuring that enterprises are kept secure as new features, upgrades, and application programming interfaces are implemented (APIs). Businesses can utilize FortiWeb to identify malicious from benign activity and spot odd or unusual behavior. See our article on using FortiWeb to fend off brute force attacks for more information.

CROSS-SITE SCRIPTING, FIRST

Information obfuscation is a technique for rearranging issues into an odd assortment of individuals. The proper security password will allow you to decipher the material. A 256-bit encryption method would require two to the power of 128 possibilities to decode, which is only generally possible on super supercomputers. Nearly all websites and online browsers make use of it. Even a system that can analyze billions of options per second would not have been able to break the authentication method's cybersecurity.

HOW DOES IT FUNCTION?

Merge hacking works by utilizing arbitrary code to steer people to a weak page. After a hack is carried out on a web device, the hacker has full control over where the software is used.

What types of cross-site scripting (XSS) assaults are there?

Cross-site scripting (Cross-site scripting) activities come in three different flavors. Some of them are listed below:

1. Conveyed XSS is a form of input validation where the prior Request message activates the computer virus.
2. The dangerous script, which is part of XSS, comes from the website's registry.
3. The defect is discovered in a programming language in Evidenced Vulnerabilities rather than for security concerns.

XSS REFLECTION

Projected Buffer Overflows are the first and most fundamental type of bridge programming. When an employee mixes information from a Response message into quick attention in an unsafe manner, it occurs. The following are some instances of buffer overflow flaws that have occurred frequently:

That seems to be in working order. /p>

RETAINED XSS

The term "stored XSS" refers to the practice of an app obtaining data from an insecure network and including that data inadvertently inside future HTTP responses.

HTTP requests can be used to send data to an application, such as comments on a blog post, user aliases in a forum, or private details about a customer purchase. In certain cases, the information might have come from dubious websites, like webmail apps that show SMTP messages, marketing tools that show social media posts, or network management tools that show packet data from network traffic.

<p>

Hello and thanks for reading my message!

</p>

DOM-based XSS, sometimes referred to as DOM XSS, happens when a client-side Java program handles data from such an untrusted source in an unsafe way, typically by publishing the data back to the DOM.

The following application uses JavaScript to read the value from a similar input field and then publish it to an HTML element:

How may XSS issues be found and tested?

Cross-site scripting (XSS) vulnerabilities can be quickly and accurately found by Burp Suite's web vulnerability scanner.

Identifying every location where the submission input is brought back in HTTP responses and running tests at each location to see if suitably crafted input could be used to execute malicious JavaScript are typical steps in manually checking for reflected and stored XSS. These insights can be as simple as a short alphabetic string.

By doing so, you can identify the context in which the XSS happens and choose an appropriate payload to exploit it. The process for manually testing for DOM-based XSS in URL parameters is similar: enter some straightforward, distinct input in the parameter, use the browser's developer tools to search the DOM for this input, and then check each place to see if it is vulnerable. On the other hand, it is more difficult to identify other varieties of DOM XSS. The only way to uncover DOM-based vulnerabilities in non-URL-based input (such as a document. cookie) or non-HTML-based drains is to spend time studying JavaScript code (such as set Timeout). Combining static and dynamic JavaScript analysis, Burp Suite's web vulnerability scanner efficiently finds DOM-based vulnerabilities.

HOW TO PREVENT XSS ATTACKS ON YOURSELF

Preventing pass scripting can be simple in some situations but much more difficult in others, depending on the user's expertise and how it maintains user-controllable data.

In general, a combination of the following actions will most likely be required to prevent XSS flaws:

When the input is received, filter it. As soon as login occurs, filter it as carefully as you can depending on whether it is expected or legitimate.

Data on the output should be encoded. Encode consumer data in HTTP responses at the point of production to prevent it from being mistaken for active content. Depending on the input context, a combination of HTML, URL, JavaScript, and stylesheet encoding may be necessary.

Make use of headers that relate to the query. To prevent XSS in HTTP replies that aren't designed to contain HTML or JavaScript, you can use the Content-Type and X-Content-Type-Options headers to make sure that browsers understand them the way you want them to.

Norms for content security One last line of defense is the Content Security Policy (CSP)

1. VIRUSES

Malware assaults are frequent cyberattacks in which malicious software infects the victim's computer and performs nefarious actions. Ransomware, malware, command and control, and other sorts of attacks are examples of malicious software, also referred to as a virus.

Malware distribution has been linked to criminal gangs, governmental organizations, and even well-known businesses. In some situations, these offenders have even been apprehended.

Because of their wide-ranging effects, malware attacks, like other kinds of cyberattacks, attract a lot of media attention.

Malware attack vectors can come in a variety of shapes and sizes.

There are three different kinds of malware attack vectors:

1. Trojan Horse: Software that masquerades as something else (such as a game or practical application) but is a means of delivering a virus is known as a Trojan Horse. A Trojan horse

depends on the target being downloaded and run by the user (usually via the internet or an email attachment).

2. Virus: A virus is a type of self-replicating malware that spreads by introducing code into other programs or files, or even specific parts of the target's operating system or hard drive. Malware spreads by injecting itself into existing software or data, which is how it differs from viruses and Trojan horses (which have intentionally put malware into one particular program).

3. Malware that is designed to spread to other systems is known as a worm. A worm actively seeks out and infects other computers (sometimes without the user's awareness), whereas virus and Trojan horse malware are constrained to a single infected target machine.

BEST STRATEGIES FOR PREVENTING MALWARE

CONTINUOUS LESSONS

Consumers are taught recommended practices for removing ransomware, including how to spot the potential infection (e.g., don't buy and activate unusual programs, and don't merely drive in "covered devices" with your machine).

Select reputable graphic and media packages.

An A/V solution, when installed correctly, will typically detect (and remove) any active spyware on a computer as well as keep an eye out for and prevent the deployment of new viruses.

Select dependable audio and multimedia packages.

Once correctly matched, a product will detect (or remove) any prior spyware on a computer, as well as look for and prevent malware acquisition and behavior when it is already present. It will be crucial to keep it current with the company's historical trends and fingerprints.

Only backups should be created and verified often.

Periodic (i.e., regular and automated) online backups could mean the difference between recovering from a severe malware infestation or virus attack and a frustrating, panicky scramble that causes serious delay and financial loss.

Adware attacks in a variety of ways and has many different forms. However, you can succeed if you make careful preparations and method adjustments. Vulnerabilities for session hijacking are rather widespread.

The following are some session hijacking flaws and methods that hackers have employed to get access to internet sessions: Data Cadger is a free tool that locates "data leakage" in online programs. It may look for unencrypted information, such as user credentials, on secure and unsecured Wi-Fi networks.

An extensive Droid program called Bionic Sheep employs "port scanning" to gather user passwords, maybe additional access, and fees from unprotected Area network web surfing activities.

A Mozilla Firefox add-on was called Fire-Sheep - Burning. By using "eavesdropping," the Fire Sheep extension allowed attackers to locate and store persistent encrypted cookies that might be exploited for credential stuffing. Due to security reasons, Fire Sheep is no longer associated with Firefox. How can I prevent someone from taking over my session?

1. Take into account adopting a shared Area network wherever practical. Never use a free area network for important tasks like banking, placing an online order, or accessing your email or Facebook sites. A hacking team may be monitoring communication at the booth next to it to look for beacons and other information.

2. Use a VPN (a virtual private network) (VPN). Use a vent connection when connected to an insecure local area network to prevent IP spoofing (VPN). A VPN hides your IP address and protects your privacy online by creating a "private tunnel" through which all of your online activity passes. If you're utilizing an OpenVPN, the data you exchange is secure.

3. Install the antivirus program on your laptop. Install and update reputable security software on your devices regularly. (You can also program it to update itself.) Security software can identify viruses and defend you against malware, including the malware that hackers use to take over your computer.

4. Keep an eye out for fraudsters. Don't click any of the links in emails if you are unsure of their legitimacy. You might receive an email from session hijackers including a link you must click

to proceed. The link may direct you to a page where you must check in to a website using a session ID provided by the attacker, or it may direct you to a page where you can download malware.

5. Whenever possible, choose to use a common network infrastructure.

Never conduct important tasks on the free Area network, including banking, online shopping, or logging into their Gmail or Linkedin accounts.

It's also possible that a hacker group is keeping an eye on the transmission of signals and other information in the adjacent box.

Always connect to the internet over a VPN connection (VPN). While using an unsecured Network, we are employing a VPN connection to protect ourselves from IP spoofing (VPN). By establishing a "virtual conduit" through which all of your internet histories pass, a VPN conceals your Email account and upholds the privacy of your online activities. The data you share is secure if you utilize a VPN.

Chapter 4:

INJECTIONS

When used in code injection, a SQL injection inserts malicious data into a website & compels it to execute specific commands, breaking the product.

A successful induction might put the entire website in danger, expose or harm data, or result in a denial of service. Similar attacks are possible due to flaws in an application's coding that allow for rejected manual intervention.

Several criteria are used to classify injection attacks.

SQL INJECTION, FIRST

A frequent attack method is SQL injection, also referred to as SQLI, in which malicious SQL code is used to control the knowledge base and access data that is not intended for display. This data may include private consumer information, use lists, and sensitive business data.

SQL is a procedure for getting ready for accessing and changing knowledge and skills to produce client information portrayals. Operations including information extraction, data deletion, and modification are carried out using SQL statements. These duties are carried out by several SQL capabilities, including searches that use the select clause to obtain data that users have entered themselves.

In an associated eStore, a typical SQL information query would look like this:

A textual query is then generated by the web service and sent to the data as a single SQL query after that:

WHO SUFFERED HARM AS A RESULT OF THE ASSAULT?

A limited group of businesses could be targeted in a supply chain assault using the Accellion vulnerability. UN organizations have used the FTC device. Financial institutions from the preceding region, the governor of Columbia, the Australian Equities and Mines Authority, telecom company Airtel, and the maker of virus defense systems Closed-loop are among the targets.

AVOIDING AND PREVENTING SQLI

There are numerous effective strategies for both preventing SQLI assaults and fending them off when they do happen.

Creating code that can recognize illegitimate user inputs is known as an authentication mechanism (also known as adequate cleaning).

Although manual intervention is frequently recommended, it rarely fails. Sorting out all allowed and unauthorized data is typically not feasible—at the very least, not without suffering a significant loss in accuracy and impairing the usefulness of the program.

Custom application firewalls (WAFs) are therefore frequently used to defend against SQLI and other internet attacks. A WAF accomplishes this by carefully weeding out fraudulent SQL queries utilizing a vast, frequently updated list of fingerprints that were painstakingly created. Such a list is typically longer than when filtering rules are applied to such routes and includes attributes for targeted attack channels.

Web server firewalls are frequently used in conjunction with several other software solutions in the environment of the twenty-first century.

A WAF may increase its cybersecurity by gathering more information from various sources.

Cross-Site Scripting, sometimes known as XSS, is (XSS)

Injection attacks also referred to as cross-site scripting (XSS) threats, involve the introduction of malicious software into a trustworthy and typically safe website. XSS attacks occur when an attacker uses client-side scripting to transfer malware to another end user via exploiting a web application. The flaws that make such attempts possible are widespread, and they can be found everywhere a web service accepts user input or correctly validates or encrypts something in its outputs. XSS occurs when an attacker persuades an internet application to send information in a format that the user's browser will understand.

Most frequently, the attacker will use a combination of HTML and XSS; however, XSS may also be used to transmit malicious files, plugins, or media material. When an online application allows information from an unreliable source to be displayed to users while not being properly on the loose, such as information entered by users into a form or passed to an API end by shopper code, an attacker is capable of tricking the application in this way.

Because XSS will allow untrusted people to run code in specific users' browsers and access certain types of information, like session cookies, and associate degrees If a body or privileged user is targeted, an XSS vulnerability might allow an attacker to demand information from users, dynamically incorporate it into online content, and seize control of a website or program.

Additionally, malicious text sent via XSS is shown instantly, whenever a website loads, or when a specific action is taken.

XSS assaults target users of an online application, and they are particularly successful because they periodically appear on a certain website.

A DIFFERENT XSS SYNTAX

A variety of various encoded and embedded versions of this software are possible. This invalidates the urgency notice (). RFC 2497 contains more information about this approach.

The following JSP script searches a database for only one operator with a given ID and displays that person's information.

INJECTION OF CODE

When an attacker takes advantage of a computer's appropriate input weakness to insert and run a computer virus, this process is known as code injection, also known as distant executable code (RCE). The syntax of the target software is modified and executed by the server-side interpreter. Internet apps are a common target for attackers because they are susceptible to harmful programming like any software that receives data from the user right away. This article discusses the causes of remote code execution problems and how to safeguard commercial web applications from them. Let's start with a straightforward example of vulnerable PHP code.

The PHP eval() method makes it simple and quick to execute string values as PHP code, which is very helpful when developing new software or troubleshooting issues. But when used with unknown inputs, it can make your software delivery obvious.

Here is a quick and dirty example of decoding a URL query using just a repeat statement, as you could have done to debug variables:

Anything you include in the online handle argument will be examined by the PHP processor. As the option name suggests, the programmer desires appropriate login information in the request message.

To take advantage of the vulnerability and insert PHP code into the application, an attacker might use the query string shown below:

In contrast, if an attack is launched, the PHP processor will run PHP info(), which will provide the attacker information about the Linux kernel, MySQL edition, and other hardware.

A competent code insertion can use the framework() mechanism to execute the command line, executing force insertion unless the kernel() technique is deactivated in PHP interpretation options (see note below). Insecure software could be used in an attack to send the activation code to a desktop website, for instance.

HOW CAN CODE INJECTION BE PREVENTED IN APPLICATIONS?

Use eval() and equivalent methods on raw input data as little as possible to avoid delicate assessment frameworks. To accept customer parameters effectively, use dialect capabilities.

Atticus treats all data as if it were suspect: Observe any areas of the application where a user may add or edit data. In addition to the typical injection pathways like XHTML pages or query terms, the program can also be added using pre-made data files, routinely updated caches, and other techniques.

Whether you are in charge of a dedicated server or not, keep the applications' interpretation capabilities to a bare minimum. This will make it impossible to insert the actual trigger. For instance, you may use the disable functions directive in the php.ini file to disable the main() method if your PHP program doesn't use it. Some of the most often disabled PHP functions include exec(), passthru(), shell exec(), system(), proc open(), open(), curl exec(), curl multi exec(), parse ini file(), and display source() ().

How Can Injection Flaws Be Found in Your Web App?

Utilizing an autonomous internet intrusion detection system is the most straightforward technique to locate an injection problem. This kind of scanning, which functions like an autonomous peri-peri program, might quickly identify threat pathways and guide you through every step required to safeguard the software.

Make sure you grasp the principles and account for all of these typical cross-site scriptings throughout the design phase because people now understand the lot more frequently employed web flaws. Even if you're not aware of how to do an effective risk assessment, humans still have you beat.

For the vast majority of injectable problems, Crashtest Protection finds, evaluates, and resolves them. You can now obtain an accurate, limitless analysis and security assessment for dangers, including attack vectors and cross-site scripting (XSS).

How many injection assaults be prevented?

To protect against code injection, one should properly design their web service. OWASP has identified several prevention techniques for software vulnerabilities, but these can also be used for other typical database assaults. These and a few additional tactics include:

Creating a point clear permit and contextually grouping user data inputs to confirm input (whitelist).

Boilerplate is used in conjunction with tailored searches to assist distinguish between the system's code and user interface and avoid taking comments for instructions.

using the system's established web service to call recorded procedures.

Due to the scarcity of special symbols, line combinations are prohibited.

By deleting any unnecessary code that could otherwise need to be protected, the final reorder map recommended by OWASPP reduces the system vulnerabilities of one's users.

imposes minimum privileged and restricted access, granting just those privileges for things like an identity that are required.

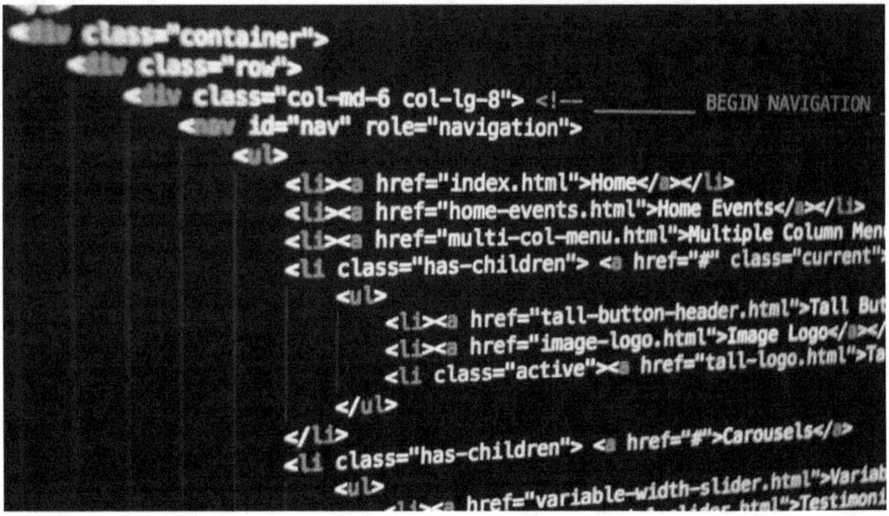

```html
<div class="container">
  <div class="row">
    <div class="col-md-6 col-lg-8"> <!--            BEGIN NAVIGATION
      <nav id="nav" role="navigation">
        <ul>
          <li><a href="index.html">Home</a></li>
          <li><a href="home-events.html">Home Events</a></li>
          <li><a href="multi-col-menu.html">Multiple Column Men
          <li class="has-children"> <a href="#" class="current"
            <ul>
              <li><a href="tall-button-header.html">Tall But
              <li><a href="image-logo.html">Image Logo</a></
              <li class="active"><a href="tall-logo.html">Ta
            </ul>
          </li>
          <li class="has-children"> <a href="#">Carousels</a>
            <ul>
              <li><a href="variable-width-slider.html">Variab
                        href="___slider.html">Testimoni
```

Chapter 5

XSRF/CSRF

Cross-Site Request Forgery, or CSRF, is the abbreviation for the things we exchange without suitable data security measures, which causes us to lose our vital data and, at that point, makes our security vulnerable. This is a web application attack where a malicious user impersonates a real user by carrying out a transaction online using the details of an authenticated person.

Any service that verifies a user generates and sends an identity token, which contains the user's transaction id, to the web client. It is referred to as the ASPXAUTH cookie in the Apache web server. The machine will now send cookie data together with each request to the website to recognize the access control. As a result, if an attacker obtains cookie information, he may use your account id to make a transfer on the website by using simple JavaScript code. Transfer data refers to sending the platform a Request message to carry out particular region duties utilizing your cookie. If a person attempts to leave the website or visits another malicious website before signing off, this could occur in the real world. Assume your website has a password reset form that looks somewhat like the one below.

A network can be attacked using cross-site proposal forgeries or cross-site scripting bridges, in which the attacker pretends to be a legitimate user with authorization. XSRF attacks are widely used to alter firewall configurations, publish unlawful content on forums, or carry out fraudulent financial transactions. It's possible that a hacked user isn't even aware that an attack has occurred. If the user finds that a low-level assault has taken place, it should only assume that damage has been done and that a repair is not possible.

By collecting the credentials for an authenticated class and subsequently breaking into a host system utilizing those credentials, several variations approach is usually beaten. A malicious user may also obtain a user's identity by tricking them into providing sensitive user information to an intrusive party over FTP (the webserver).

Numerous variations of this type of operation are conceptually equivalent to cross-site programming (Session management) operations, in which the perpetrator combines a computer virus with data exploitation to have a very dangerous impact on the data system and computer operating performance through a link on a website that gives the impression of coming from a trustworthy source. The integrated programming may be launched on the user's browser when a consumer clicks because it is transmitted together with the client's internet request.

The majority of the data can be lost once the hacker attacks our sensitive information, which enables outsiders to obtain cookies and different authentication knowledge by using a simple piece of software that runs on the targeted machine. An XSRF is a kind of different approach in the attacking system. The basic goal of a buffer overflow or central time operation is that terminal. The primary target of XSRF is the HTTP server, although average individuals are frequently hurt as a result of collateral damage. Additionally, the processor's functionality will be compromised, as well as the data flow.

Area unit assaults like XSRF are more difficult to protect against than XSS or XSS attacks. This may be partially due to XSRF attacks on area units, which are less frequent and haven't gotten as much attention. Another drawback is that it can be difficult to determine whether or not the associate degree process is appropriate. Such a user intends to propose a particular participant. Even though strict measures are typically applied to identify the person's identity trying to enter an FTP server, users may not accept any validation requests. Utilizing cryptographical identities enables continuous validation in the backend, preventing constant interruptions from authenticated users for the consumer. This section's data flow is crucial and shouldn't be disregarded.

Visitors can change this password whenever they check off and then browse a false website by completing the application form below. Keep in mind that based on the URI, the user identity will be dynamically connected to a response. Since www.yoursite.com is mentioned in the POST, the client would immediately add the cookie's information.

Although it might not be practical, requiring users to log off or requesting them not to browse certain websites may appear like preventive measures. An adversary can quickly attack a vulnerable web app using several approaches, even when the user is very cautious. We can also inspect the HTTP Appropriate to look for information to see if the request is for our website or a previous page the visitor saw before making this one. Unfortunately, we cannot guarantee that it is a successful method of avoiding CSRF as users may have blocked the browser settings option to include the Referrer header in connection requests.

XSRF OR CSRF ATTACK DEFENSE

All web stack platforms now have an anti-XSRF capability because CSRF is yet another well-known and frequently abused online safety issue.

The Xps platform represents a novel defense against XSRF assaults known as the synchronizer tokens structure. With each query, this function generates two anti-XSRF passwords and returns them to the client. These two coins are XSRF-resistant.

THE CURRENT SESSION'S ID IS:

In the form of cookies, a session identifier is transmitted, together with a 128-bit prevent cyber that must be anticipated or inferred.

A hidden form field is provided with the field token. A 128-bit security token issued for the session token is combined with the logged-in user identifier to form the value for this field. The token is created with an empty username when a user is not allowed. The IAntiForgeryAdditionalDataProvider interface allows for the expansion of the field token creation process so that more data can be included in the field token.

A hidden web form is provided with the field identifier. This column value is created by fusing a 128-bit session identification secure approach with the ability to log user IDs. If a user is not authorized, this credential is produced with an empty username. The addition of the Anti-Forgery More Data Provider interface to the field token creation process allows the field identity to now include additional data.

Within the aforementioned JavaScript help approach, a property identifier will be used as a separate output box, as illustrated below. To add validation to the Controller action method, we can embellish the action with the property ValidateAntiForgeryToken.

Chapter 6

BEST PRACTICES FOR PHP SECURITY

There shouldn't be an exception because PHP security is a serious issue and a key consideration. Given that PHP serves as the foundation of practically every website PHP programmers, on the other hand, enjoy the convenience of avoiding typical security risks. Examples of dangers include number crunching, command injection, and inter-resource spoofing. And that's pretty much it for the security features built into PHP that make it easy for website designers to safeguard their companies.

Securing websites and applications from several sorts of multicast hacker assaults may be a network designer's final effort. Your web apps should be carefully designed such that they have no known vulnerabilities or security gaps, eliminating the possibility of a hostile attack. Most of the time, manufacturers would take responsibility and do everything possible to find flaws and, if necessary, offer patches to fix the problems with the applications.

WordPress is increasingly being adopted by software engineering companies in place of their most popular software technology to create products like CMS and API generation, WordPress interfaces, and software management with the best terminal experience.

THE FINEST PHP SECURITY TECHNIQUES

CROSS-SITE SCRIPTING, FIRST

Multi shooting and port scanning are two terms used to describe each time an information system processes additional content without human awareness. You can be at risk for a SQL injection attempt whenever our web registration accepts input validation and instantly publishes these on the main page. When a malicious person adds Sgml, Jquery, or even Svg to any job website, the external computation is run.

In the image below, a template that accepts input validation is displayed.

The supporting script components will provide a basic alarm signal in the window. This situation can appear to be less severe. On the other side, an unauthorized attacker might simply steal another patient's data or personally identifiable information.

I. DATA EXPLOITATION

With full program control provided by CSRF, hackers are free to act whatever they like. With complete control, hackers can execute harmful actions on your website using infected code; as a result, cyberattacks, technological changes, and possibly other unpleasant events take place. Simply said, consumers are forced to engage in risky activities as a result of vulnerability, which can result in things like transmitting money accidentally or erasing all information without warning.

Sometimes the Cross-site scripting assault starts as soon as you click on the scammer's concealed harmful website. This suggests that even though you can find the affected applications that are buried, organizations could immediately launch either Https attack.

On the other hand, you can increase the security of your app by putting GET responses in its Address and making sure that ou pas calls are only processed by our client application.

SECOND: INCLUDING EXTERNAL FILES

The process of including distant files in your software is referred to as faraway file inclusion. Is it not significant? Therefore, why should this be of concern? because it is impossible to trust the foreign file.

It might have been altered to introduce code to your software that you don't want.

Fortunately, there is an easy fix. All you have to do is double-check your php.ini file's flag values.

3. WRITE DATABASE QUERIES IN ADVANCE.

This enables a hacker to circumvent the claim and request more sensitive information, such as personal data about entire people. An

SQL injection attack is effectively prevented by evacuating the data entered in a legal brief. For instance, the SQL query below uses user input that has not been cleaned up.

Mention things like the bind param procedure's first input.

This informs the SQL statement of the type of data that users are giving it. The first name and last name inputs in this instance are both of the String types. This additional security precaution verifies the data type that was supplied.

4. CONFIRM THE CUSTOMER DATA

Always ensure that any user input you receive through a text box is appropriate in both kind and structure. Programmers frequently use regular expressions (regex) to validate data structures like contact and birthdates. Look at the example that follows to see that the birthdate is formatted as YYYY-MM-DD.

To assure end-to-end data transfer over the internet, always use SSL certificates in your apps. A widely accepted standard protocol for transferring data securely between servers is HTTPS (Hypertext Transfer Protocol Secure). When you use an encrypted internet connection, any module can access a specific information transmission link, which reduces the risk of hackers gaining access to a company's infrastructure. All web viewers are advised to use a license key because all impacted websites may experience significant issues.

Furthermore, as it streamlines communication protocol, processing, and decoding over the network, websites that use wifi and mobile networks, including iPhone and other brands, may also be impacted.

V. SESSION ABUSE

Malicious behaviors occur whenever a criminal obtains and uses someone's child's login information because it effectively functions the same way as a password to a safe location.

When a browser and a web service start a transaction, PHP keeps the login information in a customer identification called a security address. By including the Identification in the HTTP request, you can establish a direct connection to the computer event data.

There is currently a sizable data collection that prevents Jquery from accessing the transaction identification for users running data of web or higher (who are we, really?). One might also use the set password al. (2007 approach) in a transaction ().

Identities are exposed on the webserver whenever businesses use popular online services that store log data in widely used locations, like sessions. Save any login information somewhere that no one in your routines can access, for as on a diskette or in a retail location, to get around this drawback.

TAKE ADVANTAGE OF URL MULTIPLEXING IN 6.

PHP's URL encode function aids developers in securely constructing valid URLs. According to the PHP manual, the function aids in encoding a string that will be used in the URL's query section.

Think about a situation where a URL is created based on user input.

In this situation, a secure URL might be made using the URL encode function.

VII. INSTALLING PHP APPLICATIONS THROUGH NETWORKS

Cloud storage is the final and maybe most important component in the establishment of just about any employment website. It comes after personal Scripting computers and before true platforms that offer public, subscription, or hosting services. Authorities commonly offer recommendations for internet storage services, such as Understand where you're coming from,

Different mediums, and Amazon. Smartphones are convenient, secure, and adaptable to any website or blog. Web programs typically have a protective layer to protect them from DoS, the force of nature attacks, including spoofing. Companies will need to gain a thorough understanding of Windows to develop robust web architectures for installing apps on cloud storage. This might take more time and cost millions of dollars for Windows expertise. On the other hand, you can easily and quickly develop Thunderstack workstations on the majority of the web services mentioned above thanks to the dedicated Drupal and Postgresql infrastructure technologies provided by the scope of service. This protects any PHP software without sacrificing speed against a variety of threats.

THE PHP EDITIONS ARE OFTEN UPDATED.

The most dependable version, Mysql, has been around since around August 23, 2020. The current.net framework must be kept up to date since solutions for known security problems are frequently incorporated into later versions. If you don't upgrade to the most recent stable version of PHP, terrorists will be able to exploit known system flaws in older editions.

Finally, it was our responsibility as software engineers to ensure the integrity of the agency in addition to supplying the necessary stored processes. The primary argument made by this author is the necessity of input validation. Untested manual intervention is frequently used in risk management situations. As instances of security challenges, think of distributed database integration, URL encryption, or an XSS intrusion. Each of these problems results from inaccurate human input.

```
94                          class="image/gif;base64,R0lGODlh
95          <div class="container">
             <div class="carousel-caption">
              <h1>One more for good measure.</h1>
96              <p>Cras justo odio, dapibus ac facilisis in, egestas
                .</p>
97              <p><a class="btn btn-lg btn-primary" href="#" role=
98            </div>
99          </div>
100       </div>
101     <a class="left carousel-control" href="#myCarousel" role=
102        <span class="glyphicon glyphicon-chevron-left" aria-
103        <span class="sr-only">Previous</span>
104     </a>
105     <a class="right carousel-control" href="#myCarousel" role=
106        <span class="glyphicon glyphicon-chevron-right" aria-
107        <span class="sr-only">Next</span>
108     </a>
109   </div><!-- /.carousel -->

110
111   <!--Featured Content Section-->
112     <div class="container">
113       <div class="row">
114         <div class="col-md-4"></div>
            <div class="col-md-4"> <h2> FEATURED CONTENT </h2>
115         <div class="col-md-4"></div>
116         <div class="col-md-4">
```

Chapter 7

SESSION MANAGEMENT

Over the past several issues, we have already looked at the good, the bad, and the ugly of our long-standing and illustrious connection with the Modbus system. In conclusion, Telnet's ability to maintain a consistent connection, especially in demanding programs, is by far its greatest benefit. On some of the more great apps, we pay a price for this ease in the form of dropped connections, insecure discussions, and dated-looking facades.

By reducing our dependency on permanent connections, web forms that use HTTP, as opposed to Modbus, may provide us enhanced security, state-of-the-art client experiences, and, very importantly, increased stability. Although all of these aspects are admirable, it's crucial to keep in mind that internet interactions are temporary, which means that each request to the client establishes a new relationship with the service.

Without any context, an app has no way to know if it has encountered you before. For instance, we typically start by logging in to the client when visiting our apps, especially those that are used frequently. Think about what would occur if you logged in and the computer ignored you immediately! Because this is exactly what happens when communicating online: the host keeps forgetting who you are long after the sale ends.

The conference component cannot guarantee that only the Associate who planned the event will have access to any insights gained during or after a discussion. Based on the value attached to the chapter, more protections are required to keep it secret.

It is important to evaluate the transaction's information's relevancy and put any necessary security measures in place, although doing so typically comes at a cost, such as decreased consumer comfort. For instance, temporary use or passwords must always be disabled to stop hackers from using a straightforward social marketing technique. Analytics must be allowed in full on the purchaser component in this case; otherwise, transactions would not be able to be completed.

There are various ways that login information can be disclosed to a third party. Flash injection, transaction identification on websites, protocol sniffers, equipment access rights, and so forth. A compromised identity exposes all underlying shares associated with that ID to a payment gateway.

Addresses with transaction Identifiers to start. The universal resource identifier and the User-Agent may be located in the referrals records of the external third party if there are linkages to external websites or resources. Furthermore, many common attackers may be able to hear data transfer.

If they are not secured, soon-to-disappear can be delivered across the connection in text format. The answer is to implement Transport Layer Security on the website and make user compliance a requirement. HSTS must be put into practice. Session management is a complex chore to do, and when we employ evaluation, it gets even more so. Dealing with such circumstances over the long term may be very challenging. On the other hand, the PHP programming language offers a good example of how the state may be kept in a web-based application. Though there are other web technologies and languages to choose from, we will concentrate on PHP for the time being because it is not only effective but also surprisingly simple.

In terms of MultiValue, think of this parameter as a huge mass of allocated memory space. The size of this block can then be nearly infinitely increased by adding other factors, which in turn can store further variables. Although the implicit array is a wonderful feature of the PHP language, it disappears when the script's memory is exhausted, just like all other variables. However, with session management, the $_SESSION variable does not disappear until we instruct it to or until the customer closes the window, whichever occurs first.

Once the software has run its course, PHP saves the parameter to the hard drive and loads it again the next time the transaction is required.

A little example of how this might be utilized On line 3, the script calls the session start method (). Believe it or not, this is all that is required to make PHP support session management. Once the session has begun, we can utilize the $_SESSION variable just like any other variable, with one significant exception: anything we leave in this variable after our script will remain accessible the next time we run it (or any other script on this site that makes use of session start) ().

In part 6, the set() command is employed to determine whether a parameter from the $ Conversation bucket is present. This will show whether we are beginning this event for the first time or picking up where we left off with just one. We can be sure that this is our first interaction with this property by checking to see whether our $_SESSION collection contains an entry for "numbers," in which case we can set it to 0. We can raise the integer and then repeat (broadcast) the number once the majority of this cleaning is finished.

The first time this code is run, it will output one. If you reload the page, it will print two times, then three times, and so on. Every time the website is reopened, this series would start over at 1 because PHP retains the identifier even when the website is active. PHP will establish a fresh connection and start over if you leave and restart the computer.

However, there are times when we want our code to permanently save data, even if the machine is rebooted. demonstrates this code as

a small modification that enables this capability. The session id ()
function allows us to identify our account, and anyone with access
to this ID can view our session variables. Since the consumer is
concerned about security, this should make you sweat a little because
it instructs the script to share the same information with others so
they can update it if necessary as well as save your data between
browser restarts.

How concerning are websites that keep data even after page restarts
while keeping personal information separate from yours? The code
shown illustrates how this might work. When humans initialize all
of our other period parameters, they may also install a cookie on the
web browser containing its current session token (line 15).

For instance, the computer would clear the cache in 24 hours, but in
the meanwhile, it gives us a place on your desktop to store the session
ID.

We run the danger of a data breach whenever the user enters user
input or information that is saved on the online computer. That is
significant to remember A skilled programmer might easily change
the PHP session token by changing a cache, and the application
would be completely unaware of the change. They do, however, have
several protections in place to lessen this risk.

We have added a layer of security by saving the user's Port number
in the session parameter on the web application. Following the
moment PHP imports the account, if the Internet protocol of the
experience does not match the user's location Internet address, we

may delete their current connection, unset (erase), and start a completely new meeting for the user based. The advantage is that it was unusual for an attacker to access the user site from the same IP address as the original user.

However, it would have a drawback if a user's site visitor often viewed a site from a device having such a variable Internet address (as might be the case).

A person may worry about the effectiveness of that kind of state administration, in which data is stored on disc and periodically retrieved, in addition to security. It has the potential to be spectacular, which is surprising. However, in a typical software, especially one that is widely used, the user would not typically maintain gigabytes of data in RAM either. The user will not intend to utilize or recover gigabytes of data in the variables on every connection.

Access control in PHP generally makes handling information simply. A network error is much less likely to happen in a jumble of terminated encounters because multiple references are received from or saved to memory for each transaction. By using HTTPS to access the program, the user could obviate any risk and obtain the highest level of safety.

In the end, such technology might enable us to reach the broadest possible audience while enabling us to use some of the most sophisticated touch screens available.

Without a doubt, society's governance is unimportant. Everything is currently open as well.

Therefore, what have users got to lose?

Is it accurate to say that sessions are maintained using just one parameter? "How could one element be so potent?" One parameter might store all of the data in the user's program despite having the ability to expand because it is an additive matrix and can carry any quantity or database schema (storage limitations taken into account).

Chapter 8

PHP SESSION

WHAT EXACTLY IS A PHP SESSION?

When engaging with a program, one launches it, makes changes, and then dismisses it. This is analogous to a Session. Either a machine or a human can recognize you. It maintains data that is helpful and customer-friendly, so it would keep good track of when clients start using the program or get closer to pausing their use of it. The HTTTP URL strangely does not control the environment of status, so the site host is still unaware of who you are and what you are doing. This is an issue on the internet.

This issue is resolved with temporary parameters, which save user data that can be reused across multiple pages. Until they are deleted by the user, temporary values are retained on the computer.

Because the web and browser identifiers store information about a certain client, it is possible to get such data from all sites through a single software.

ESTABLISH SESSIONS

How are sessions created in PHP using various techniques?

One must first comprehend "what is the session" to comprehend what it means to start or construct a session. Cookies are used to store data, but there are certain security issues. Making the program unusable is potentially risky because the majority of crackers can recognize and alter cookie content. The server receives cookies data right away when a user requests a URL or refreshes their browser.

The browser will lag since the cookies include more information. The performance of the website will degrade as a result. PHP sessions were developed to address these issues. The Php session was created using data that was hidden on the user network; nevertheless, this does not suggest that the user is using a specific device.

Each user of identity in this PHP environment will have a special number known as a client identity. This type of client identity will enable the user to connect each advertisement to everyone who uses the internet, including social networking, private information, and secret information.

In this PHP environment, each client would have a unique identity described as a client identity. It will be possible to connect every user's private information, such as posts, images, social networking, and other things, to the computers using that additional ID. The directory location of the PHP session file is specified in the "PHP.in" file, also known as "suasion. Save path."

A new session will be started or an existing one will be restarted by the function session start (). To check whether the PHP session was created, at least some data has been saved.

Here, the session is just created using the session start () function.

This will solely help with the session's PHP code development.

The following code will also print nothing in the browser because it is an empty session with no PHP functions or code.

The syntax for starting/creating a session is as follows:

Example #1: Launching the "session start ()" function with a single line of PHP code.

The information is then entered, including first and last names, ID, favorite color, favorite animal, favorite area, favorite hideout place, and so forth, after the transmit PHP code has been started "

"Captain Kumar" is represented by the session variable $_SESSION["firstname"]= "Captain Kumar"]= "$_SESSION["firstname"]= "Captain Kumar"""

The first session's "first name" key and "Captain Kumar" value are both present. Everything at the conference was the same way.

To know more about or make changes to the data that was already saved when the creation took place, the third PHP code now accesses the started data. The values of all the session variables and keys, as well as any information we want to know or change, will be published here. The text that follows the echo will be displayed, followed by the value of the session variable, a line break, and then all of the session's keys, variables, etc. will be printed before the program terminates. We can write the code in several HTML files and run it in the browser after

STARTING THE SERVER TO ACCESS THE VARIABLE VALUES OF THE STARTED SESSION.

Output:

Captain Kumar is his given name.

He goes by Sake King.

His identifier is 1473.

Blue is my favorite color.

OX is one of my favorite animal names.

HIS PREFERRED LOCATION IS THE HIMALAYAS.

Anantpur is the name of his favorite hide-output location.

Example #2: Establishing a session with scant information.

Using the fundamental function "session start ()," we establish a session and then store the "first name" and "last name" keys with the values "Pavan Kumar" and "Sake" in the PHP source code.

This program will output nothing even though its session contains data with variables like first and last names.

Because we aren't accessing the file using PHP's echo statement, when these sessions use simply the session's variables to generate or insert data into the file, nothing happens.

Example #3: Accessing a PHP session that was created using data.

In this software, a PHP session is also started using the session start () function. The preset function echo is then used to create the text, after which the session's variables—such as first name and last name—are employed, and their values are written on the screen. The welcome phrase will then be printed using the echo statement.

Obtain Sessions

Java can save any data in process settings, but you should first get to work. You must use the PHP conversation begin () function to start a new session. Customers would create new sessions as a result, and everyone would receive a personal ID. The essence of how the PHP code informs about the new session is defined in the following code.

The connection starts () function first checks the availability of an identifier to see if a transaction is currently in progress. The transaction properties are set if one is discovered; otherwise, any with a comparable session ID is created.

Your datasets can all be kept in the $ Workout [] large universal collection as public keys. Throughout the sessions, the saved data is accessible at any time for viewing. Take a look at the software below, which generates a new account and modifies three session parameters. To obtain the session data we defined in our previous example from any other page on the same web domain, just recreate the session by running session start () and then giving the appropriate key to the $_SESSION associative array.

Data saved in sessions can be easily accessed by first calling session start () and then providing the pertinent key to the $_SESSION associative array.

HOW CAN I RETRIEVE VALUES FROM A SESSION IN PHP?

The value of a session variable can be obtained using the global variable $_SESSION. In the example below, you'll start a new session using a variable that contains your name. Now that the variable has been set, you will utilize another file to access it.

Simply set the name variable, make a new file, then enter the following code to access it.

```
<?PHP
  session_start();
?>
<html>
<body>
<?php
echo "User is: ".$_SESSION["name"];
?>
</body>
</html>
```

HOW CAN I ACCESS THE SESSION VARIABLE IN PHP?

By executing the period to begin () and then sending the value to the $ Sash array list, a program can be retrieved. Establish the connection (); state the child's name again: ["Pseudonym"] $_SESSION How can I use a session variable on another page?

Each page or PHP file that requires access to the session must include the session start function (). The easiest way to accomplish this is to make a header. Include/require the PHP file at the top of each page that is common to your site.

How should the session variable be used in another PHP file?

To do this, use $_SESSION['word'] = $word. In the other file, immediately before the PHP "tag," you must also use session start (). To access the previous variable, use $word = $_SESSION['word'].

a destruction Session

To retain user information and make it available across the web application, sessions were developed.

As a result, the server can identify the application's visitors using the special session identifier.

The session is over when a person logs out or closes the browser window.

The following functions can be used to end a session:

A single session variable can be deleted using the Unset () function. A parameter called the target variable is necessary.

Session destroys () - This function erases all previously set session variables. The usage of any parameters is not required.

You can manually end a session even though the web server will automatically do so when the browser is closed. This can be done with the aid of two functions.

Session destroys (): This function eliminates all session variables.

Unset (): When this function is invoked, just the specified session variable will be deleted.

Use the transaction unset () technique to delete some of the trial's parameters, but not all of them. Could you all take a moment to consider when to end the accounting control you established earlier? Example: Destroying a Session Variable with unset ()

If any additional variables are present, only the counter variable will be terminated.

Use the discussion terminates () technique to end a PHP session.

This technique can be used to eliminate all temporary variables in a specific line without taking into account any parameters. If you merely want to remove a certain clinical property, use the method, for instance () method.

Designers are eliminating a customer inside the displayed example.

The temporary integer will first be verified by humans, who will then discard it to end the game. Show the transaction again, however this time it will be a null collection because the transaction doesn't quite happen.

Ex#1:Code:-Output: The sessions removed the collection ()

They start and set the count parameter to 0 at the beginning of something akin to the program. The next step is to check if any session variables have been set. This count parameter number is increased by one if a meeting named webpage visits is initiated; otherwise, the counted constant parameter is presumed to be one.

Example#2: Code: The session has to be erased when a user logs out or exits the application. A session is automatically destroyed when a user closes her browser. This happens because when the user's browser is closed, the PHPSESSID cookie on their computer expires. The creation of a robust web application requires the use of PHP Destroy Session.

Simply including the code to end a session is required as a good web programming practice. If your web program must log out after a specific amount of time, such as in the case of Online

Banking or any service that relies on financial transactions, it will be handy in several situations. If a user forgets to log out, this is done to protect her data.

Another situation is when a consumer places an order on a shopping website but does not yet leave the page, in which case the customer's shopping cart needs to be cleared. In conclusion, ending sessions will help to safeguard the private, financial, and confidential data of website visitors.

The following things happen when a PHP session is ended:

All variables and data from the session are eliminated.

Global session variables and associated cookies are not erased at the end of the session.

Detroit session does function

A session is destroyed by calling the session to destroy a function in the PHP language (). This function doesn't require any parameters. It just removes the session data from storage when called in the PHP script as explained below.

When a session is removed, the session data is still kept in the super global array $_SESSION. The superglobal $,_SESSION is cleared only at script completion. "S Session" By initializing super global data with an empty array just before the script terminates or the user logs out, super global data can be deleted.

After all of this, the PHPSESSID cookie may still be present on a user's computer to end a session, but it will be empty. On the user's subsequent return to the page, the session can be restarted in her browser even if the PHSESSID cookie is empty. The session must be ended by deleting the session cookie from the server and the browser to prevent this. The example that follows exemplifies this.

PHP immediately ends the session when there is a timeout or when a user leaves the website. A session as a whole, or individual variables whose function has been completed, may need to be explicitly destroyed.

When a user signs out or closes the application, the session must be ended. As soon as a user closes her browser, a session is instantly terminated. This occurs because when the browser is closed, the PHPSESSID cookie on the user's PC expires.

A crucial aspect of developing a dependable web application in PHP is session destruction.

The code to end a session simply has to be added as per acceptable web programming practice. If your web programmer must log out after a specific amount of time, like with Online Banking or any other service that relies on financial transactions, it will be useful in several circumstances.

If a user forgets to log in, this is done to protect her data.

When storage files are used, sessions destruct () will delete the connection data. The experience file will, however, only be retained on the server until trash removal takes it away. To ensure that the user's cached program is deleted, you must use sessions destroy ().

The id must have been upset since it ended the session. This data must always be erased if the cookie is used to transmit the identifier, which is the case by default. Set data () may even be used in this situation. Is erasing the PHP session necessary?

Although it isn't necessary, it nonetheless violates your privacy to leave some material here when the designers aren't around.

Although period destructs () can also be used to halt an identity, they shouldn't send any of the parameters for the chapter or the conversation token, according to the proof that was formally documented. After a specific amount of time, how do you end a session?

It can be done by choosing the outbox or by closing the account; after that, a predetermined period expires. Any newly created account will expire in 1440 seconds, often known as (24*60), or in 24 minutes. But sometimes we might have to change the flow of time. Does session destroy remove cookies?

To conserve performance, session destruct () periodically executes rather than instantly deleting session data maintained on the server for that session's id and requests that the client erase that cookie.

Which variables are erased when the page is closed?

If pushchairs are used for the event instead of cookies, the process starts. Every time the window is opened, your temporary identification is removed, thus your account will be active until they shut off the computer.

How do I get rid of session variables in the best way possible?

By using the command session unset, which clears all session variables, you can clear the session variable.

(For previous deprecated code, using $_SESSION = array () would be comparable.)

With the command unset ($ SESSION['Products']), you can only change the session variable's Products index. Session destroys — This command clears all session-related data.

What is the most efficient way to send sessions when cookies aren't present?

Do you recall ever seeing a message on a website informing you that cookies are being used and giving you the choice to reject them? A user can easily turn off his computer's use and storage of data.

How would the application software be able to determine the session's identification id if passwords were not used? Nevertheless, it appears that there is a decision.

You can use a constant SID for this. It is defined at the beginning of the session. If the user agrees to the use of cookies, the user line is null. However, the SID constant will have the formula session name=session id if the user rejects cookies. You can register and save variables using this form forever.

chapter 9

HOW SAFE ARE PHP SESSIONS?

The internet method and Transmission Control Protocol were designed from the ground up to be connectionless. This suggests that every approach to the browser is unique and already has all the data needed for the host to deliver the intended webpage. The website does not monitor the information or status of the vision; instead, each signal supplied by the user to the service may be treated separately.

Internet applications need a way to store user data, from the ability to track user logins and shopping carts for business owners to longer-term data like prior purchases or discussions in networking site apps.

TCP and any programs developed on top of it must therefore come up with ways to deal with HTTP's innate marginalization. The most well-liked substitute is using a website. PHP sessions appear to be the best online programming language available today. We'll examine PHP session strategies, PHP identity privacy, and how to protect PHP session cookies in this post.

We'll examine potential hazards as well as practical fixes for keeping PHP transactions secure.

Thanks to its protocols, HTTP appears to have been scalable from the beginning. This suggests that the consumer flags might be utilized to make Web apps and responses more complicated.

Each query or response contains a preamble element, which might contain several pieces of information.

Cookies were first established by the Internet Engineering Task Force (IETF) as an addition to HTTP, and the definition has since changed to become RF 2295, also known as the HTTP Intercrosses Communication Method.

Cookies are a mechanism comprised of HTTP headers that may be used by websites to save data (state) in HTTP clients, according to the Internet Engineering Task Force (IETF). This enables the server to preserve a transaction—a domain-specific background—over succeeding HTTP requests.

The host can reproduce variables like the customer's trip and a grocery cart site identity by using the mouse cursor (the client) to transfer comparable data to the server during subsequent calls.

Analytics come in two flavors: transient cookies and permanent muffins. Cookies are transient symbols that exist only when a user is browsing. The cache in the address bar contains them. Tickets don't even have an expiration date because they become invalid as soon as the active computer session ends.

Session cookies have a predetermined expiration date and are designed to be utilized for a specific length of time.

PHP attempts to include a feature that is essential for modern websites: persistent data over several visits to a website's pages. On the other hand, there is debate concerning the appearance of PHP IDs.

Efficiency and scale concerns may occur because PHP identification information is by design entered into a file on the client and the directory is closed throughout function takes.

While skipping the store for sites with PHPSESSID might necessitate missing the shop for the actual website, archiving sites with the PHPHSSISD token set could seriously damage a domain.

PHP PRESENTATION VULNERABILITIES THAT AREN'T PATCHED

In terms of security, PHP periods are slightly more advanced than a system where all persistent data is stored in passwords. A benchmark ID for a server-side identity file is all that the PHPSESSID token includes. The default setting for a path to save meeting papers in PHP may be found in the php.ini system settings as "HST saves path = "/tmp". This suggests that session files could potentially be compromised by other users.

This issue gets even more serious when people realize that the majority of scripting language blogs are currently housed on network servers with several tenants.

The most frequent transaction vulnerability is a backdoor.

Attack via Session Hijacking When a malevolent party gains unauthorized access to the subsequent debit, working data theft occurs. The hacker has to get hold of another user's session key. Using this ID, the attacker should then be able to see all of the transactions made by other users. The service simply needs the session Token to grant access to the right client.

The Id might be obtained through prediction or guesswork (brute force), but hijacking it may be the most likely scenario.

The likelihood that a brute force attack or guessing the ID will succeed is substantially higher.

A participant's Session ID can be obtained by an intrusive party via several techniques.

What actions is the attacker permitted to take while using a session that has been hijacked?

The service gives the hacker full control of the user's account when they get access to a legitimate customer's account. As a result, the Id may be compared to a key that grants access to a residence even if the user is not the owner. Due to the regular usage of login information to track users and transactions, the adversary may occasionally be granted access to the compromised website.

It is important to recognize that issues with PHP exercises are not specific to the language once we have discussed the numerous steps that people can take to stop hackers from stealing PHP accounts.

People are not a PHP problem; both of these systems use comparable security measures to thwart other network threats.

Where can we find some fundamental procedures that will protect us from threats of credential stuffing?

The attacking approach known as an XSS (Cross-Site Scripting) attack lacks a session-specific defense. The webpage must forbid performing any input validation on the client's PC. In the simplest terms, all users that are obtained by forms, GET parameters, or other methods must be sanitized before being used. This is a common cybersecurity approach that guards against additional risks and threats of a similar nature (e.g., SQL injection). htmlspecialchars() and strip tags are the only two fundamental PHP text sanitization techniques (). In contrast to htmlspecialchars (), which turn special characters into HTML objects, strip Tags () just eliminate all HTML tags, including special symbols.

Session Sidejacking can be prevented by employing encryption methods over the entire demand interface. There is a potential that the transaction data will be revealed even if the link is adequately encrypted.

For instance, if a visitor/client has already created a website and Internet Explorer has an open connection with PHPSESSID pastry, the visitor may occasionally consider accessing the same webpage via cellular internet. In this case, when John clicks on the empty weblink (without a security policy arrangement), the search engine would then forward it to the vulnerability, HTTP edition of the email at first. However, in and of itself, this won't be forwarded to the HTTPS variant until after that (301 redirects).

Account Constant focus will be most frequently used in Web address access control, which occurs when an intrusive user persuades a legitimate user to create a preset Login. This shows that the URL's Get parameter has been updated to contain the Identifier. One possibility is to trick the victim into signing up using a hidden web form in the form the attacker constructed.

A session can be corrected in several ways by manipulating cookies. You can find more Account Fixation attacks in the Vulnerability Database (OWASP).

Session. The main PHP option related to this security hole is to use trans sid. "Invisible session IDs" are enabled when this option is set to 1.

Predicting sessions — To prevent this, web apps must create page content that is sufficiently long to be unpredictable throughout (entropy). Even while modern PHP (7.3.1+)'s normal PHP parameters were unquestionably secure enough, if the software needs persistent bespoke ways, it's best to be cautious. You can see the whole list of PHP environment settings.

In cases when the device type does not support data, PHP will be permitted to pass its session token in URLs.

For security purposes, this is typically set to 0, which precludes opaque SIDs. When utilizing trans id is set to 1, for instance, we run the risk of anyone (for instance, using a shared computer) being able to access the sessions by looking for the URL containing your session token in the address bar history or by looking through records of computers inside the intermediate. A PHP option is a session. Use software that is accessible to many people and all primary customers (with standard protocols enabled). This option explicitly forbids the usage of URL components as transaction IDs. As a result, employing PHP sessions safely in addition to Encounter.

PHP connections can only be as secure as the application that uses them. PHP identities will give users a phrase that may be used to identify themselves (a "session ID"); but, if an attacker intercepts the string, they can then impersonate the victim.

CAN YOU MAKE USE OF A PHP SESSION?

Encounters are saved on the local computer of the customer rather than merely on servers. Find the phpstrid tag under your domain name in your cookies. Computers may be hacked, and this type of hacking technique is used frequently.

Identity protection in PHP is a perennial source of concern. For PHP web apps (like WordPress or the Vue.js framework), native PHP discussions are frequently insufficient or unreliable. As a result, some, like Visual Studio Structure, choose to produce highly customizable remedies while forgoing PHP meetings, while others, like Blog, choose to build customized solutions on top of PHP native exercises. Whatever course of action we choose, we must be aware of any dangers to PHP performance and security.

We covered several fundamental PHP transaction security issues to be aware of in this book, along with PHP security suggestions. Because this is more of an insight than a comprehensive list of all the constraints, we suggest visitors conduct their independent research.

```php
<?php
$login = isset($_POST['login']) ? $_POST['login'] : '';
$password = isset($_POST['password']) ? $_POST['password'] : '';

if ($login == '') {
    header('Location: session.php?error=1');

} elseif ($password != "toto") {
    header('Location: session.php?error=2&password'.$password);
} else {
    session_start();
    $_SESSION['login'] = $login;
    $_SESSION['password'] = $password;
    $_SESSION['logged'] = true;

    header('Location: session-bienvenue.php');

}

?>
<!doctype html>
<html>
    <head>
        <meta charset="utf-8">
        <title>Interagir avec le visiteur: Les sessions >> PHP/MySql Initiation</title>
```

Chapter 10

BEST PRACTICE FOR PHP SESSION MANAGEMENT

Since its initial release in late 20, PHP has developed into a paradigm for DB connectivity and even a platform for users to create websites-based internet applications.

Php is an open-source program that may be used to make static websites more dynamic by processing input in the user's backend and returning or outputting the results on the screen.

Everybody who contributes meaningfully is at least aware of the problems with establishing websites and internet applications. You consciously make your program accessible to everyone who comes along, everywhere on the planet. Possibly PHP's initial fault was prioritizing ease of use.

THE TEN BEST STEPS WEBSITE OWNERS MAY DO TO SAVE THEIR SITES ARE LISTED BELOW.

1. Session protection for PHP
2. the visual mistake that was turned off III. restricted file uploading
3. PHP must protect sensitive data.
4. Access URL open ought to be disabled
5. Close all magic quotes.
6. Register global has to be disabled.
7. Use trans sid needs to be turned off.
8. The php.ini file must be used correctly.
9. Check PHP settings with "PhpSecInfo."

I. SESSION PROTECTION FOR PHP

Numerous web apps contain sensitive information that has to be updated to stop abuse due to session-related flaws.

To achieve the session detailed below, a few things and actions must be taken:

Use Tools to identify people or carry out important activities. Visit to form an essential aspect for a free HTTPS registration.

Reset the client id if the protection level changes (such as logging in).

The session id for each query can be generated at your discretion using the session recreate id rule.

Set a timer to halt sessions after a certain period.

Keep the client's usual procedure in place rather than employing international registration. This means that you should not save any private information, such as a password, in the cache.

Look at the variable. Data theft is slightly hampered as a result of this. Additionally, you may find someone's IP address. However, this causes problems for users who, among other things, have a changing Port number as a result of task scheduling on numerous online sites.

You can restrict access to events that only affect a single data structure or use a personalized session management system.

Encourage requiring registered users to resubmit their user credentials for important actions.

II. DISABLED VISUAL ERROR

utilizing two separate techniques to look for PHP errors while your website is active. Another incredibly hazardous option is to show genuine issues on the website (which can be viewed from any Surface app), or you can enable error tracking, which would record the issues to a particular file (can be found in the file).

The book would explain how to disable visual issues in PHP.ini and would also enlighten readers on how to change issue-reporting parameters, construct error reporting, and use the mini set () method to troubleshoot PHP problems on a website.

Screen errors must be disabled in the php.ini file when the person's website is active due to security concerns.

Whether or whether error messages are shown in the client is controlled by its illustrated errors element. These notifications should always be disabled because they frequently provide important information about how your website is configured. This command must always be set to "on" in the PHP ini file. It will highlight any errors, particularly lexical and parsing issues that are hidden by merely calling the t method in PHP code. The file's PHP can be found under the heading "imported information files" in the output of the phpinfo () method.

This command in the ini setup should be modified to off if the web service is running. The PHP. etv file's parameters were set as follows:

The option can also be disabled in Apache's httpd. cent or home file to quiet every PHP error:

Most errors are noted using the error sign, which is often set to /PHP/null. This means the ability to report errors will be removed. If errors are permitted, they are recorded in a file at the site where the error occurred.

If someone wants to display an error to a certain page when they want it to be shown on the site- openly intended to show on a specific single page- they can use the default () library. the following syntax is provided by the php.net library for the given issue and its variables, which may be added at a higher level of PHP by utilizing the error problem attribute:

'display errors', '1' in ini set(string $varname, string $newvalue);

III. THERE ARE LIMITATIONS ON FILE UPLOADING.

If someone is unwilling to use a feature properly, it is best to turn it off. Any person can use and exploit them based on weak security and person's careless attitude toward the security issues of files and always seem vulnerable about the file structure, making it easier for attackers and hackers to use the file by sending harmful PHP code and injecting them into any web page. This can be advantageous for the hacker, and they may simply take advantage of the feature of a file that was uploaded and left for open access.

To disable this, open the php.ini file and edit the directive, which is fully described and coded in the file's basic form below. This file is crucial to utilize.

Unless using the SharePoint command, make sure to change the default temporary location for sharing files.

This may be done simply by editing the following file:

The following link can be helpful when uploading a file that contains a large database and can be limited to a particular amount since it allows you to control and reduce the file's size.

It is the responsibility of the individual to check that the uploaded file is in the appropriate format. to confirm that the uploaded file is functioning properly. The user can use the following command to determine whether the uploaded file is in the correct format or not and to assist with error analysis.

IV. PHP MUST PROTECT SENSITIVE DATA.

If the PHP code is somehow not put up correctly, it includes several characteristics that could be used to take over the website. Disabling hazardous methods such as exec (), past.how(), shell exec(), and others are simple and may be done by editing the php.ini file and using the disable functions command.

Anyone may disable specialized roles for security reasons by following the disable functions guideline.

To do this, open the PHP. idi file and add the following commands to the new list: exec, pawswssthru, shallow exec, system, prows open, power, curl exec, curl multi exec, parse ini file, display source = close parameter. You can use any word processor, such as Microsoft Word or Vim (on a Linux system).

V. ACCESS URL OPEN OUGHT TO BE DISABLED

The declaration enables the various PHP files to retrieve data from distant websites.

FTP HTTP.

When a hacker can alter the parameters for such processes, they might run their local scripts using a website they manage as the parameter, which is known as remote server inclusion (RFI) Because of this restriction, techniques like included () and necessary () can import and provide the status from remote URLs, endangering every page. Modify your directive in the intended file as below indicated to disable the equation provided to deactivate these directives.

off allow URL fopen

By using a directory structure rather than an Address to ping file retrieve contents ($ WOST['URL]);, anyone can easily access another person's files.

The httpd.conf file in PHP has the following configuration:

php admin flag allow url fopen Off

Many of the cross-site scripting flaws reported in PHP web apps are caused by allowing URLs to be accessible and inadequate data screening. Users must always deactivate that rule for their protection.

6. CLOSE ALL MAGIC QUOTES.

This directive can only be deactivated by the operating system. The magic. quotes gpec option was developed to aid in the defense of websites against SQL injection threats. Every piece of data received through GFET, POSTT, or COOKIES is effectively subject to adds slashes().

For instance, PHP automatically removes the inverted commas and saves the output as "hey year hub" when a user types "hello yeahhub" (in quote marks) into an HTML form.

HTTPd.conf or access files may be configured in Apache to perform the following functions:

VII. REGISTER GLOBAL HAS TO BE DISABLED.

The register global command is disabled by design. It is important to think about how using the register global command may affect privacy.

A PHP option called registered global transforms the elements in a $ Demand collection into constants. Users that upload a number in a kind using POST or GET will be able to access that data using a PHP script method with the same name as the entry course.

Change the price of the previous rule's price to Go off in the PHP.in file to deactivate a rule.

Write the following command in an htaaccess file (or hhttpd. conf) when using PHP as an

Apache extension, limiting this to the file one would like to access.

When the utilize trans SSID option is selected, PHP sends the login data via the address. Your app is hence significantly more vulnerable to node capture attempts. Data theft that is done ethically involves stealing a real client's session token and using it to impersonate the customer. When the identity ID is given in a frame and the query is carried out via a secure network, it is secure (i.e., SSL). In reality, it makes these users susceptible to having their sessions hijacked by anyone who: sees the URL without the user's knowledge, acquires the user's Address, or receives the URL from the user's browser history.

THE USE OF THE PHP.INI FILE MUST BE ACCURATE.

Making a php.ini file is a straightforward process. In a word, the PHP.in file adapts the server's parameters to the specific requirements of a website.

Users can alter several options in the PHP.in file at any time, including, among other things, the

RAM activation restriction and the huge file uploading capability.

The quickest way to determine which directory PHP.inii is in is using the "search" line, however as we've already discussed, there are typically several PHP.inii folders on a website, so this option would still be beneficial since we already know the file's position.

VIII. CHECK PHP SETTINGS WITH "PHPSECINFO."

A method similar to phpinfo() called phpSecIInfo reveals private data about the PHP context and offers improvements. Although it is not a replacement for safe practices and does not perform some coding or application audits, this can be a useful component of a thorough cybersecurity plan.

Chapter 11

MANUAL FOR PHP

This is the final chapter of the book; throughout the earlier chapters, we looked at several PHP security-related issues and their effects.

In the current internet infrastructure, PHP security has emerged as a global strategy. We have proven that PHP is stronger than other languages via examination. It uses well-known methods and has robust security protocols. PHP protocols enable us to safeguard our data, and they are a huge aid and necessity for us to protect our most sensitive information online. Throughout this book, we have seen a variety of core libraries that can be helpful and supportive for us as we project our private data.

 As we go through this book, we learn about PHP sessions and how developers of the PHP programming language were able to make them extremely helpful and secure for clients and users. In the present era, PHP is a prominent language with significant data security and safety features. The majority of networks use it globally and it has highly sophisticated administration to secure user personal data. PHP protects the data and code. The most crucial aspect of PHP is that it secures data because it isn't displayed in the browser and may be turned off using various minor codes that we have covered in previous chapters.

 Although PHP still has some weaknesses, we must rely on them because they depend on the programmer.

The problem can arise when a developer creates code, which could result in suffering and the loss of important data.

Avoid all possible hacker access points whenever a code developer makes writing errors that make the code extremely exposed since the problem can be caused and data can be misused. PHP has been demonstrated to be extremely secure and has a high action against hackers. All of these criteria were thoroughly covered in an earlier chapter.

Popular open external source high-level programming language PHP (Hypertext Preprocessor) is well suited for web design and can be integrated into HTML.

That is excellent, but the question is still unclear because it doesn't say what it implies. This chapter will give a brief overview of PHP's manual and its operation. The fundamental operation of this security language is simple to comprehend, as we will see in the example that follows when we look at the system's coding.

LET'S EXAMINE THE CODING FOR:

PHP knowledge gives HTML an appropriate tool that executes "things" (in this case, print "Hello, I am a Ph script!") rather than a lengthy list of instructions to create HTML (like in C or Perl). Does specific computation begin and finish instructions follow the PHP script? With the aid of PHP and?>, users can switch between "PHP mode" and "normal manner."

The best thing about PHP is that it not only offers a straightforward module for new users but also proves to be useful and collaborative for experts. It gives experts more sophisticated tools so they may work on more complex issues and avoid encountering major difficulties while doing their respective jobs. Therefore, PHP is quite user-friendly and has built features that can help its users. This book just expands on security in the PHP manual. Therefore, incorporating the file in PHP is the first step. To include just one file, use this code. Take a peek at the PHP coding below. The file's placement or inclusion is determined by the index.

What implications does this have for application? If the needle was not found in the haystack, an array () returns either FALSE (if the needle was not found) or TRUE (if the needle was found in the haystack). The first parameter, the needle, is designated as "mixed" since it can take on a variety of shapes. A single scalar value (such as a string, integer, or float) or a group of scalar values (such as a string, an integer, or a float) could make up this mixed needle (what we desire) (array).

The array we're looking for, haystack, is the second input. The third optional argument is the strict parameter. You may find all of the optional arguments in [brackets]. The documentation states that the strict option's default value is the Boolean FALSE. The instructional page for each function has information on how to utilize it.

How safe is my software application? is a question that has baffled software engineers for years. A full-fledged software-as-a-service may now be produced and released as the foundation of a comprehensive product or business thanks to advancements in modern web application development.

Your product can only be used to interact with data accessible through your web service API, a mobile app, or a browser. Unfortunately, the areas where your product and data are subject to security threats, criminal breaches, and data theft increase as these modern software media expand into more complicated platforms. When you receive an email or text message from one of these people, it isn't them sending it; rather, it's a computer virus file that has spread all of these messages across the network, including links from government organizations, spam/junk mail from other people's spam lists, and hackers who have hacked into your system and obtained sensitive information or files you were unaware were even there. All of this suggests that neither our personal information nor, more importantly, our vast amounts of data are secure.

How secure is the information we share on social networking sites? This is a very difficult question. Developers must always keep security in mind when creating Internet-based applications and while writing code. Most inexperienced developers are indifferent about security issues when working with PHP. The security of any transaction involving money or other sensitive information should always be a top priority.

Unlike other attacks, XSS assaults are conducted on the client's end. A JavaScript script that is going to submit a form is prevented from gathering the user's data and cookies by using the most basic XSS tool.

XSS tool protection is more difficult than SQL injection tool defense. The websites of significant corporations have been the subject of XSS attacks. Although PHP has nothing to do with this assault, it can be used to filter user data and protect it. The main goal is to remove HTML components, especially the tag, to filter user data. Harmful data is sent to the server through the post for general JavaScript front-end verification because it is impossible to know the user's actions, such as turning off the browser's JavaScript engine.

The information sent to each PHP script must be checked on the server side to prevent XSS attacks and SQL injection. It's best to leave it alone. The file is organized as follows: globals register = Off. There will be a significant security risk if this configuration option is enabled. As an illustration, there is one process.php. The script file will add the data that has been received to the database. The following forms may be used to collect user input data: Name: "username"; type: "text"; size: "15"; maximum length: "64";

This method of sending data to process.php causes PHP to establish a $username variable and pass the values of the variable to the process.php file. For any post or get request argument, this variable is set. If the display is not initialized, the following problems will develop: Data injection into SQL When utilizing SQL statements to manage databases, security must be taken very seriously because users may insert specific statements to change the intent of the original SQL statements. This is comparable to the following example: Two steps need to be taken to prevent SQL injection attacks:

ENTERING INPUT SETTINGS TWICE ENSURES ACCURACY.

It is always necessary to use special characters, such as the single quote mark, double quote mark, and back quotation mark.

REAL ESCAPE STRING FUNCTIONALITY IN MYSQL

However, based on my development experience, don't activate PHP's magic quotes. Since PHP6 disabled this functionality, it is now necessary to escape strings whenever feasible.

USE SAFE HTML TO PREVENT XSS ATTACKS.

Although the XSS prevention described above is straightforward, not all of the user's tags are protected. There are numerous ways to submit Code generators without using the search function in the interim, and there is no way to get around this problem.

Even while improved security is always available, no program can currently ensure that it won't be attacked. White lists and black lists are the two categories of security protection. The white list requires less effort and time.

TO SECURE DATA, ONE-WAY HASHING CRYPTOGRAPHY IS UTILIZED.

Because of one hash protection, each user's password is unique but unchangeable. The system is unaware of the prior passphrase, and only the end-user is aware of the password. A credential attempt has the benefit of keeping the attacker from accessing the original data.

Cryptography and hashing are not the same things. Since hashing is bidirectional and cannot be reversed in the absence of decryption, the originality of the hash value can be guaranteed even when two different strings produce the same result.

It is feasible to decrypt the hash value generated by the MD5 algorithm. You can find additional cryptographic hashing languages online.

locking up data The MD5 hash method can display data legibly, but to decrypt the user's credit card information, it must first be encrypted and stored.

The mcrypt module, which contains over 30 encryption methods and guarantees that only the encryptor can decrypt the data, is the best method to use.

The attacker can break the ciphers and gain access to the bank if they have both the data and the key. As a result, we must MD5 the encrypted key only once to ensure security. The encrypted data generated by the mcrypt function is binary data, thus putting it in a database field will also cause problems.

These integers are converted to hexadecimal for storage using base64encode.

This concludes the book's content and introduction chapter. I sincerely hope that the information in this book will be useful to you in your studies or professional endeavors. In the coming chapters, we will describe each topic in the book in more detail and detail, so that you can see how it relates to other chapters. The book's content will undoubtedly advance and strengthen the concepts.

When a site's content is not password- or Internet protocol-protected, there is no need to use the configuration settings. One can utilize CGI if a web service doesn't enable referrals or doesn't have a way to inform the PHP binaries that the demand has been securely redirected. To compel a redirection, use the force redirect directive.

The PHP manual discusses a variety of topics that are crucial for comprehending and learning the fundamentals of PHP.

Because they enable web pages to provide flexible content that changes over time, databases have grown to be essential components of every browser application. Organizations should seriously consider safeguarding databases since they may include extremely sensitive or private information. Php offers security to a variety of websites, including HMLT, and it's also highly beneficial for databases because it differs from other languages, such as JavaScript, which is weak and frequently finds data on the browser.

149

PHP protects data and takes all essential precautions to prevent data exploitation in the modern world. It is without a doubt a very strong foundation for security-related elements. PHP offers a range of techniques and procedures that we can use to protect vital information from various hackers.